D. Travers Scott
Editor

Strategic Sex
Why They Won't Keep It in the Bedroom

*Pre-publication
REVIEWS,
COMMENTARIES,
EVALUATIONS . . .*

"**S**trategic Sex doesn't offer writing about sex so much as it shows us writing as sex—a seductive, presumptuous, and erotic come-on to the brain and other organs. Imagine a long summer of surprising encounters, of sudden sex in public places, with every imaginable complication. As thrilling as gossip, as sexy as good porn, and far smarter than the average bear, this collection proves that D. Travers Scott is as talented and astute an editor as he is a writer."

Matthew Stadler
Author, *Allan Stein*

"**S**mart, sexy, and full of surprises, D. Travers Scott's *Strategic Sex* is wilder than a roomful of drunken sailors. These often startling and always provocative essays explode popular assumptions about the imagined boundaries between gay and straight, male and female, and—most important—private and public. Sex is never 'just sex.' In expanding our awareness of why sex can never be reliably consigned to one or another neat little square, *Strategic Sex* is key reading for everyone, and exceptionally entertaining reading at that."

Steven Zeeland
Author, *Military Trade*

More pre-publication
REVIEWS, COMMENTARIES, EVALUATIONS . . .

"**F**rom the gym and the rock club to the university and perhaps nirvana, these writers canvass the American scene, constantly surprising the reader with the artful wit of their investigations. The topic of sexuality is used to explore and explode the many barriers marring contemporary discourse—not only those between classes, races, and genders, but between the mind and the body as well. Rarely has a book made for such good reading either with both halves of your brain or with just one hand. This is sexual play as it should be: edgy, committed, and vibrant.

At a time when we are asked to believe that the Sexual Revolution has ended in defeat, *Strategic Sex* reminds us that we have not yet begun to understand the myriad ways our lives have been transformed."

Nayland Blake
Artist, Curator, and Writer
Brooklyn, NY

Harrington Park Press
An Imprint of The Haworth Press, Inc.

Strategic Sex
Why They Won't Keep It in the Bedroom

HAWORTH Gay & Lesbian Studies
John P. De Cecco, PhD
Editor in Chief

Strategic Sex
Why They Won't Keep It in the Bedroom

D. Travers Scott
Editor

Harrington Park Press
An Imprint of The Haworth Press, Inc.
New York • London • Oxford

Published by

Harrington Park Press, an imprint of The Haworth Press, Inc., 10 Alice Street, Binghamton, NY 13904-1580

Cover design by Marylouise E. Doyle.

Library of Congress Cataloging-in-Publication Data

Strategic sex : why they won't keep it in the bedroom / D. Travers Scott, editor.
    p.   cm.
    Includes an index.
    ISBN 1-56023-969-7 (hc. : alk. paper).—ISBN 1-56023-970-0 (pbk. : alk. paper).
    1. Sex. 2. Sex customs. I. Scott, D. Travers.
HQ12.S74 1999
306.7—dc21   99-29520
                                                                                                      CIP

for Scott O'Hara

CONTENTS

ABOUT THE EDITOR

D. Travers Scott is the author of the acclaimed novel *Execution, Texas: 1987* and co-editor (with Richard Labonté) of *Best Gay Erotica 2000.* A first-place winner in *Steam* magazine's first Porn-Press Awards, his writings on sex and culture have appeared in anthologies such as *Gay Men at the Millennium, Best American Gay Fiction 2, Obsessed, Best Gay Erotica 1996 and 1997, PoMoSexuals, Contra/dictions, Reclaiming the Heartland,* and *The Mammoth Book of Gay Erotica.* In addition, his writing and performance scripts have appeared in periodicals such as *Harper's, International Drummer, New Art Examiner, Blithe House Quarterly, High Performance, Women & Performance, Black Sheets, Paramour,* and *Holy Titclamps.* Mr. Scott has also presented his solo and collaborative performance work in Brazil and locations throughout the United States. For over two years he served as Managing Editor of *P-form,* an international performance art quarterly.

Contributors

Ron Athey is a performance artist and writer, bound for most of his life in Los Angeles. He and his performance troupe, Ron Athey & Co., have toured a trilogy of body-extreme theater in the United States, Europe, and Mexico since 1992. One day he hopes to finish writing a book of stories and recollections based on his Pentecostal upbringing (and the accompanying perversion), *Gifts of the Spirit*. In 1998, the documentary *Hallelujah! Ron Athey: A Story of Deliverance* was finished, filmed in collaboration with director Catherine Gund Saalfield. Currently, Mr. Athey is doing a world tour of his first solo performance, *The Solar Anus*.

Jennifer Natalya Fink is the author of a novel, *The Mikveh Queen* (for which she won the 1997 Dana Award), and is co-editor of *Performing Hybridity* (University of Minnesota Press, 1998). She is a professor at Pratt Institute and New York University. Her new novel, *Burn*, concerns America's favorite pastimes: communism and pedophilia.

Karen Green was co-editor of *A Girl's Guide to Taking Over the World* (St. Martins, 1997) and co-publisher of the zine *Pucker Up*. Her short stories have been published in *Best Lesbian Erotica 1996* and *1997*, *Pucker Up*, *Time* magazine, and various self-published works. When not working at *The New York Times* or hosting literary events in New York City, Karen is finishing her novel and a book of short stories.

Marti Hohmann is a Web site editor for the Crescent Publishing Group. Formerly Editor-in-Chief at Masquerade Books, she is the translator of *Dolorosa Soror,* a novel by Florence Dugas.

Katinka Hooijer is a women's health activist and is organizing a nonprofit holistic health agency. She holds an MS in Cultural Anthropology from the University of Wisconsin-Milwaukee, where she currently teaches courses in feminist rhetoric and pornography. She plans to edit an anthology of work concerning issues of chronic illness, female subjectivity, and female sexuality, and is looking for contributors (and a progressive publisher). She can be reached at Katinka@csd.uwm.edu.

Jaron Kanegson's poetry and essays have appeared in *Countering the Myths: Lesbians Write About the Men in Their Lives, Telling Tales Out of School: Gay and Lesbian School Days,* and community publications such as the *FTM Newsletter.* Jaron has performed poetry and other stuff in various places, including at LunaSea Women's Performance Project . . . along with partner Gretchen . . . as discussed in her essay!

R. R. Katz was born in Lecce, Italy, in 1961. He moved to the United States at a tender age and grew up mostly in New York. He wrote and illustrated comic books with lots of naked people in them from age eight. He majored in Asian Studies at Brown University and got an MA in the same field at Yale. Those degrees turned out to be fairly useless and have not catapulted him to a position of national prominence, although he did develop a reputation in the university dining hall basements as a skilled dishwasher while he worked to pay tuition. He is a painter and a writer, and has been combining those two media for the last few years, with shows at Sherkat Gallery, New York University Gallery in New York City, OMS Gallery and Gallery 33 in Portland, Oregon, and Project 416 Gallery in Seattle. His writing and/ or painting has been reproduced in several recent Sun and Moon Press books, and featured in *Don't Panic Magazine.* He produces a zine and e-zine at http://www.teleport.com/rrkatz under the name of Flotsam Press.

Dorian Key is a nice, perverted boy from the Bay Area. Her work appears in *Best Lesbian Erotica 1998, Wicked Women,* and *On Our Backs.*

Kevin Killian is a poet, novelist, critic, and playwright. His books include *Bedrooms Have Windows, Shy, Little Men, Arctic Summer,* and *Argento Series.* With Lewis Ellingham, he has written *Poet Be Like God: Jack Spicer and the San Francisco Renaissance* (Wesleyan, 1998), the first biography of the important U.S. poet.

T. A. King teaches queer and performance studies at Brandeis University. His book *Queer Articulations: Men, Gender, and the Politics of Effeminacy in Early Modern England* will be published by the University of Wisconsin Press in 2000. With Moe Meyer, he is editing *Pleasure Praxis: Essays on Contemporary Gay Performance.* His essays have appeared or are forthcoming in *Monstrous Dreams of Reason: Writing the Body, Self, and Other in the Enlightenment, The Politics and Poetics of Camp, Presenting Gender: Changing Sex in Early Modern Culture, TDR (The Drama Review), Theater Insight: A Journal of Contemporary Performance Thought,* and *Viewing the Male: The Image of Manhood in Early Modern Literature.*

Jayson Marston is a writer living in Los Angeles whose work has appeared in *The Unreal Guide to Los Angeles* and *Drummer.*

Scott O'Hara is rentable at your local video store in twenty-six different skinflicks; he also founded and for three years edited *STEAM (A Literary Queer's Guide to Sex and Controversy).* He is the author of *Do-It-Yourself Piston Polishing (for Non-Mechanics)* from Masquerade/Badboy, and *Autopornography: A Life in the Lust Lane* and *Rarely Pure and Never Simple: Selected Essays,* both from Haworth/Harrington Park Press. His play, *Ex-Lovers,* premiered in January 1998 as part of the twentieth anniversary season of Theatre Rhinoceros, San Francisco. He died in 1998 from complications due to AIDS.

Carol Queen is the author of *The Leather Daddy and the Femme, Real Live Nude Girl,* and *Exhibitionism for the Shy,* and co-editor of Lambda Literary Award winner *PoMoSexuals.* She holds a doctorate in sexology and likes to take her clothes off when she uses it. Visit her at www.carolqueen.com.

Michael Scarce is the author of two books, *Smearing the Queer: Medical Bias in the Health Care of Gay Men* and *Male on Male Rape: The Hidden Toll of Stigma and Shame.* He is a doctoral student in medical sociology at the University of California, San Francisco. Focusing on gay male sexual health, cultural studies of science and technology, and perverse poetry, his work has appeared in such publications as the *Journal of Homosexuality, POZ* magazine, and *Diseased Pariah News.*

Lawrence Schimel is the author of the short story collection, *The Drag Queen of Elfland*—which was a finalist for the Lambda Literary Award, the Firecracker Alternative Book Award, and the Small Press Book Award—and of *The Erotic Writer's Market Guide 1999,* among others. He is also the editor of more than twenty anthologies, including *PoMoSexuals: Challenging Assumptions About Gender and Sexuality* (with Carol Queen—winner of a Lambda Literary Award), *Switch Hitters: Lesbians Write Gay Male Erotica and Gay Men Write Lesbian Erotica* (with Carol Queen), *Two Hearts Desire: Gay Couples on Their Love* (with Michael Lassell), *The Mammoth Book of Gay Erotica,* and *Things Invisible to See: Gay and Lesbian Tales of Magic Realism,* among others. His stories, essays, and poetry have been included in more than 100 anthologies, including *Best Gay Erotica 1997* and *1998, Gay Love Poetry, The Mammoth Book of Fairy Tales, The Random House Book of Science Fiction Stories,* and *The Random House Treasury of Light Verse,* among others. He divides his time between his native New York City and Madrid.

Theresa M. Senft is a doctoral candidate in the Performance Studies Department at New York University, where she writes about sexuality and technology. She is the co-editor of a special issue of *Woman & Performance,* titled "Sexuality & Cyberspace," and is at work on her dissertation, "Feminettiquette: Feminism, Performance, and the Internet." Theresa's work has appeared in *The End(s) of Performance* (NYU Press), as well as several online Webzines: *STIM, Barnes & Noble Online,* and Prodigy Internet's *Living Digital,* where she is a weekly columnist.

Simon Sheppard is a nice guy, but a bit of a sexual sadist. His work has appeared in dozens of anthologies, including *Best Gay Erotica 1999, 1997,* and *1996, Best American Erotica 2000* and *1997,* the Fantasy and Horror volumes of *Bending the Landscape,* and *Male Lust.* He is, with M. Christian, co-editor of *Rough Stuff: Tales of Gay Men, Sex, and Power* (Alyson, 2000). He would like to thank Tim S. for providing inspiration and ejaculation.

Wickie Stamps is a writer whose published works appear in numerous anthologies, including *Flashpoint* (Richard Kasak Books), *Close Calls* (St. Martin's), *Brothers and Sisters* (Harper San Francisco) *Switch Hitters* (Cleis), *Once Upon a Time* (Richard Kasak Books) and *Sons of Darkness* (Cleis). Wickie, the former editor of *Drummer* magazine, has recently launched her own film production company, titled murder/mayhem.com.

Tristan Taormino is the author of *The Ultimate Guide to Anal Sex for Women* as well as publisher and editrix of the pansexual zine *Pucker Up*. She is also the editor of the *Best Lesbian Erotica* series, and co-editor of the erotic collections *Ritual Sex* and *A Girl's Guide to Taking Over the World: Writings from the Girl Zine Revolution*.

Sally Trash is a critic living in Vancouver, BC. Her favorite subjects have been sexual art and porn, class cultures, and the name-calling that goes on around sexual imagery, prostitution, sexual rights, and S/M. In her time off, she lives by the motto "Indulge in what you enjoy and ignore the rest." She enjoys writing, public speaking, editing (she was the former editor of *Lezzie Slut* magazine), photographically incarnating a female Robert Mapplethorpe, filming porn, and being bisexual.

Preface:
Sex and the Steam Engine

Strategic Sex asks an unusually clear and direct question about sex: Why? Sex is typically regarded as unconscious and instinctual, a blind force from the nether regions of id and libido. The contributors to this book, however, are not operating blindly. They think hard about sex: before, during, and after. Yet their analyses do not throw a wet blanket of sociological constructs or psychoanalytical mindfuck onto the party. They strive to keep sex's power intact. They want to examine this vital force, to learn its potential and effects. As eighteenth-century inventors saw the power of the steam engine in a teakettle's rattling lid, these writers see powerful energy sources in the boiling forces of sex. Here they recall, relate, dream, and imagine ways of harnessing that energy, putting it to work. Theirs is sex with a purpose, sex with direction: strategic sex.

But the genie must be out of the bottle in order to work. Critique and dialogue, sharing of discoveries, and the passing on of history require a public forum. One-to-one communication behind closed bedroom doors is not often the most effective method of disseminating information, building skills, or sharing ideas. Hence, a great deal of strategic sex is public sex.

Public sex, however, is all too often dismissed as mere perversion, with irrational, useless motives: For attention. To get off. Addiction. Insanity. Such dismissal belies the great anxiety public sex arouses in a culture soaked in fear of the body and all things sensual. Western culture weaves vast veils and barricades of "impropriety" to keep these Dionysian forces plugged up. Nonsensical and contradictory social codes of behavior are instilled from birth onward. Legal systems resort to absurdly specific degrees of penile tumescence and aureole visibility to build a definition of indecency. Far from moral absolutes, the way these proper/improper boundaries are defined and maintained is thickly intertwined with class and privilege. Dominant power structures seek to inhibit and control information that threatens their hierarchy. "By the time recorded history began," writes sex historian Reay Tannahill, "authoritarian societies had already discovered that by disciplining sexual relationships it was possible to exercise a control over the family that contributed usefully to the stability of the state."*

Public display of private realities can disseminate information and facilitate change. The contributors to this book aim to do just that. Educator and activist Katinka Hooijer's essay reveals the dangers of privatized knowledge and hidden sexuality, as she finds herself another chapter in the history of women shafted by the medical establishment, in part due to social constructs of propriety and perversion. In publicizing some of the most private aspects of her life, she strives to help truncate that history. Californian "boydykes" Jaron Kanegson and Dorian Key each address the body as well, questioning and exploring its role as the public site for gender. The manipulation and alteration of the body is explored both by Ron Athey and Lawrence Schimel. Body-extreme performance artist Athey traces the history of his tattooing, from a public pronouncement of sexuality to a historical marker. Prolific erotica writer and editor Schimel explores the quasi-private space of the gay gym as affording a unique environment where public specimens of a sex-defined social group are developed for presentation to each other and to the outside world.

Several writers explore sex's place in the public forums of education. The late porn star, radical sex activist, and influential gay writer/editor/publisher Scott O'Hara reflects on the sexual education in his own childhood and adulthood, and imagines that of future generations. Marti Hohmann discusses with legendary porn star and performance artist Annie Sprinkle her efforts to teach nongenital orgasms and the heightened awareness they can spur, especially to communities of women. Sexologist, author/editor, and performer Carol Queen describes her peep show work and performance art as logical extensions of her human sexuality studies and outreach efforts. Medical sociologist Michael Scarce invades the private space of a university men's room with a public discourse on rape prevention to engage his target audience with their social guards down. Writer and scholar Jennifer Natalya Fink's fiction articulates a dizzying vision of child-

---

*Tannahill, Reay. *Sex in History*. Lanham, MD: Scarborough House, 1992.

hood sexuality colliding with the codes religion and adult society attempt to instill and enforce.

Public sex as a thread in the fabric of community building and social reimagining is explored by several contributors. Scholar T. A. King explores S/M subcultures, searching for culture, community, and meaning. Visual artist Rafael Katz examines differing races' and cultures' sexual stereotypes of each other as experienced during his years studying in Taiwan. Los Angeles writer Jayson Marston's characters use sex to defuse societal racial tensions by enacting them in exaggerated, consensual sex scenes. Simon Sheppard and Karen Green, both writers and editors of cutting-edge, pansexual erotica, each explore sex oscillating between personal gain and manipulation of others as private social circles and public performance stages overlap.

Perhaps one of the most visible forms of public sex is the commodified sex industry. Former *Lezzie Smut* editor Sally Trash delivers a how-to for women on taking control of porn videos not necessarily made for them. Wickie Stamps explores her responsibility as former editor of *Drummer,* one of the longest-running gay S/M porn mags, where historical preservation runs afoul of contemporary commercial censorship. Technology theorist Theresa Senft delivers a moving portrait of commodified phone sex playing a crucial role of emotional sustenance in daily life. Prolific erotic writer/editors Tristan Taormino and Kevin Killian both reveal insights and experiences gained while working as porn models and performers, and how they put those revelations to work.

This is not another warm and fuzzy erotica collection, academic jargonfest, or uptight porn debate. Nor is it starry-eyed, sex-positive cheerleading. Like sex itself, this book is thrilling and depressing, dark and transcendent, paradoxical and contradictory. It is fiction and nonfiction, queer and straight. Boundaries are blurred and definitions are messy—again, like sex itself. *Strategic Sex* is a book about questioning, thinking, and exploring. It is not about definitive answers or pronouncements. Rather than resolve, it hopes to deepen the mystery of sexual energy and, in so doing, inspire more exploration, thought, and discussion. And more sex.

D. Travers Scott
Seattle, Washington

Acknowledgments

Heartfelt thanks for all your support: Ellen Blum, Bill Brent, Alex Cigale, Cleis Press, David Eckard, Jennifer Natalya Fink, Dan Garlington, Karen Green, Bruce Karlen, Jim Ochsenreiter, Steve Omlid, Bill Palmer, *P-form Magazine,* Carol Queen, Randolph St. Gallery, The Robert J. Schiffler Collection and Archive of Greenville, Ohio, Lawrence Schimel, David H. Serlin, Wickie Stamps, Tristan Taormino, Ken Thompson, Mitchell Waters, Steven Zeeland, and everyone who wrote, submitted, and/or revised but couldn't fit into the final version of this book.

This book developed from the "Performance and the Pornographic" issue of *P-form Magazine,* #39, Spring 1996, in which different versions appeared of "Moby Dick in the China Sea," "Interview with a Metamorphosexual," "Slipping," "Porno-formance: Some Notes on Sex as Art," and "Pentimento of a Rock-Hard Cock."

A version of "Porno-formance: Some Notes on Sex as Art" has also been previously published in *Real Live Nude Girl,* by Carol Queen, Cleis Press, 1997.

"Slipping" first appeared in *two girls review,* vol. 1 no. 2, 1995/1996.

"Wholesome and Natural" first appeared in *Rarely Pure and Never Simple: Selected Essays of Scott O'Hara,* Harrington Park Press, 1999.

"Hot Lights" first appeared in *Gerbil,* no. 4 (1995).

"Exercises in Manual Dexterity: Making Porn Videos Work for Lesbians" first appeared in *Lezzie Smut* issue no. 8, 1996, pp. 44-45.

"Caution: Sharp Object" first appeared in *ChickLit 2,* edited by Mazza, DeShell, and Sheffield (FC2, 1996), and an excerpt appeared in *X-X-X Fruit,* no. 2.

"Under My Skin" first appeared *Honcho,* vol. 50, no. 1, January 1997.

"Girlfriends, Boyfriends, Dykes, or Fags?" first appeared in *InsideOut Youth Magazine,* no. 11, May 1996.

Pentimento of a Rock-Hard Cock

Wickie Stamps

Old paint on canvas, as it ages sometimes becomes transparent. When that happens it is possible, in some pictures, to see the original lines: a tree will show through a woman's dress, a child makes way for a dog, a large boat is no longer on an open sea. That is called pentimento because the painter "repented," changed his mind. Perhaps it would be as well to say the old conception, replaced by a later choice, is a way of seeing then seeing again.

Lillian Hellman, Introduction to *Pentimento*[1]

A lot of men, usually older, complain that *Drummer* isn't what it used to be. "*Drummer* was better in the early years," they say. *Drummer* was something. It was a part of something. They tell me *Drummer* was not, as it is now, a sterile image of a time and place. "*Drummer* used to be about real men's lives," they say. A way of life. Now, like a faded photograph, *Drummer* vaguely reflects what sex—and life—was like. Before now.

Men, often older leathermen, call and Frank, the receptionist, gives the calls to me. There is an urgency in their voices, desperation crackles through the line. The request is always the same. Someone needs to write about the way it was. About the past. Someone needs to remember, needs to tell the stories. Their stories. Record the history. Show the images.

Someone must tell everyone about the way it was before . . . now.

I listen to these men with their deep voices. They tell me about bars, and clubs, about fisting, about a way of life. I listen as they lay out a past rich with raw passion, now littered with fading voices. They tell me that *Drummer* has changed and is not the way it used to be. I listen to them talk about a world I've never known.

1

Mineshaft. Folsom Street. The Slot.

"Yes, yes," I say, my willingness to listen the only thing that holds them above their despair. I ask them to write down their stories and send them to me. As quickly as they can. Their urgency now mine. My promise to read what they write all I have to offer.

I hang up the phone. I sit in my chair and stare at the phone. I am, as always, stunned by their urgency. Wondering if I am now living on a dying planet that has yet to build its time capsules so that someone, somewhere will someday know the way it was. Before . . .

"Nice dick," I hear Mike, the art director, say from behind the partition. And I am gratefully pulled back to the moment. I push myself out of my chair and wander over and stand behind him. We both stare at the slides that litter his light table. I glance over at the scanner and stare at the image of a large dick on a larger, muscular man being scanned onto the screen. I am grateful for the distraction. Away from the voices.

"Christ, he's hot-looking," I say as I turn and stare through the magnifying glass at a man on the back of a pickup truck fucking another man in the ass.

"We can't print them," Mike says as he wanders back over to the scanner. "Penetration."

I examine a dozen other slides and motion to Mike to come back over and look. He and I agree that three of them might get past the printers. Maybe Mike can airbrush out the penetration.

Drummer cannot show bodily fluids. Piss. Cum. Or penetration. Mike jokes that we cannot show sex anymore. And soon it will be the cocks that disappear from the pages.

By now Frank, the receptionist, has wandered over and peers over our shoulders. Frank just loves big dicks and always comes around the corner of the partition to see what Mike has found.

"He's huge!" Frank proclaims and blushes at his own desires.

Mike, Frank, and I laugh and I wander off, my eyes glancing at the stacks of photos that cover the table near Mike's desk. Faded photographs, photographic archives of men. Of cocks. More and more as I walk from my desk to Mike's I stop and pick through the stacks. I look at old photos and see men caught in a snapshot having sex. I think of the men on the phone. I walk over to Mike's light table and stare at more slides from recent shots. I look at the photos and see models, poised, feigning sex. Hinting at the way things were.

Drummer must be less raw. More suggestive. More and more dollars pouring into legal fees. To interpret laws that are burying cocks, suppressing cum. Emasculating *Drummer.* Breaking our spirits. Softening our readers' cocks.

I walk away from the light table and stand in front of the boxes of photos piled in the corner. I think about the voices on the phone.

Mike likes to dig up old photos from these stacks. Stacks no one has time to organize. The first photo Mike showed me from these archives was of a young man, standing in an abandoned tenement, perhaps in New York. He was standing by a window, shirtless with just a pair of jeans on. It was as though the photographer had caught the young man in the midst of his life. Ready to have sex. To do what *Drummer* can no longer show.

We get young men with sweaty palms in all the time who want *Drummer* to capture them on film. There is an eagerness in their eyes as they sit waiting for Mike to talk to them. Mike doesn't like to ask them to pull down their pants and check out their dicks even through he knows he needs to. After all it's *Drummer.* Mike's always polite to the young men with eager eyes and unseen cocks.

Invisible, fading.

I pause and pick through a few photos. I stare at men with hard cocks; I am mesmerized by the muscles. I think of the young men who come into the office, so eager to be seen . . . by anyone beyond themselves. Who desperately want other men, anywhere, to see their cocks, their bodies. Their cum.

I stare at men's bodies.

I stare at hard cocks.

I've started lugging old *Drummers* up from downstairs. Slowly I flip through the yellowed pages looking for what is there. What everyone says was the way things were. I stare at the men, I read the stories, I try to find the world that is trapped in the voices of the men on the phone.

"Wickie, phone call," Frank says. I put down the magazine and walk back into my office. I stand in the doorway to my office and stare at the phone. I look over at Mike, who is busy staring at the scanner. I look back at the phone. And wonder why I want to cry.

At *Drummer* I am inundated with manuscripts, letters, photographs, and illustrations. They pile up on my desk, they spill onto the floor.

So many are bad, missing the point. Recently, I came across a quote by writer Carson McCullers from her book *The Heart Is a Lonely Hunter*. I often apply it to the limited work—and images—that come across my desk. In her quote she is talking about the people of a desolate town who are coping with a harsh winter: "And by habit they shortened their thoughts so that they would not wander out into the darkness . . . beyond tomorrow."[2]

But sometimes in a line or paragraph of a letter, entire manuscript or photo of some bleary-eyed man standing in a bar, dick out, drink in hand, I am suddenly lost again, like in that scanner or those old photographs. Lost within a world of raw sex, unbridled passions. At that moment their work comes alive and so do I. With photo or text in hand I wander over to Mike. He turns from the image before him and asks, "What have you found?" I hand him my treasure and wait for his response. Sometimes he rejects my offering. But more often he says in his quiet way, rubbing his chin as he scans the work, "Not bad, I think we can use it."

Sometimes I feel as though I am a woman without eyes, without touch. My eyes are the eyes of the men on the phone. My eyes are Mike's eyes. Looking for images of a world that is his not mine. Mike and the men on the phone gently take my hands and place them on a world of throbbing, rock-hard cocks, they turn my head and point it toward a world with big-dicked, hairy men, thousands of men, in bathroom stalls, in back rooms. A way of life that is theirs not mine.

Mike tells me that the series of photos of the men on the back of the pickup truck had to be pulled. Too extreme. We would not get them past the printers.

I stand beside Mike and watch as an image emerges from the scanner. More cocks. No cum. Never any cum. Just cocks. Dry cocks. We can still show cocks. Today.

Maybe, this time, maybe in this picture we will find what we are all so desperately searching for. And I can finally say with great joy to someone, somewhere, perhaps those men on the phone, that I have at last found, refound, unburied the world that they, and now I, am so desperately, urgently seeking.

Each day I walk to my mailbox and open my mail.

Hot, horny man seeks . . .
Slave seeks . . .
Master seeks . . .
Boy seeks . . .
Dear Sir . . . I am seeking . . .

It seems as through everyone is seeking something they've lost. Seeking something they do not have.

Mike's leaving *Drummer.* He's going to work at another publication. "I think they can show real men there, just guys," he says as he, in his chair, scans in yet another old photo of a guy getting fisted. He turns and looks at me and gets upset because I have started crying. He comes over and gives me a hug. I rest my head on his shoulder. When I stop crying I lift my head and look over his shoulder at the image that is appearing on the screen. Two men, one leaning over with his ass spread, the other with his hand going into the first man's ass. I am mesmerized by the scanning and the image before me. I am the editor of *Drummer* and I cannot remember if I have ever seen such rawness. I am the editor of *Drummer* and I cannot remember if I have actually seen an image of fisting. I am the editor of *Drummer* and I cannot remember if I have ever seen two men actually having sex. I know I must have but, at this moment, I cannot think. I cannot remember. I wipe away my tears and stare at the image emerging before me.

"It shows penetration," Mike says as we stand side by side and gaze at the men appearing on the screen before us.

Every image that appears in *Drummer* must be documented with the model's name, address, photo ID, and any aliases used. Images that even hint at sadomasochism increasingly put us at risk of raids, arrests, and seizure of all property. The paperwork is endless. The documentation is burying us alive. Fear gnaws at our creativity. Stress saps our energy.

"I'll stylize it," Mike says and suddenly walks off, grabs another old photo from the jumble of pictures, and slides one in front of me.

It's an old photo of a guy in a uniform. Not a model. Just a guy. "What do you think? I just found this."

"I love it," I say. Mike and I stand side by side and stare at the old photo. Behind us the scanner fades out the details of the ass fucking.

Sometimes I feel as though I am a woman without eyes, without touch. My eyes are the eyes of the men on the phone. Looking for images of a world that is not mine. My hands are now the hands of the men on the phone. Gently, they take my hands and wrap them around their world of hard cocks. Dark alleys. A world seething with hot men. A world that is theirs not mine. A world that existed before now. I am the editor of *Drummer*. I am the eyes of what was.

Mike was going to participate in a small *Drummer* photo shoot. I overheard him telling Frank that, in the photo shoot, he wanted his dick out. Frank thought it was a great idea. Of course.

Mike never did that photo shoot. He didn't think he had a good enough body. I was sad because I wanted a photo of my friend Mike. With his dick out. Standing there with a drink in his hand. I wanted that photo. So that Mike, and all that he taught me, would never become a pentimento in my mind.

NOTES

1. Hellman, Lillian. *Pentimento,* First Edition. Boston: Little Brown & Co., 1973, p. 3.

2. McCullers, Carson. *The Heart Is a Lonely Hunter.* New York: Bantam Books, 1940, p. 169.

Dialing

Theresa M. Senft

There are three things to do in Buffalo: watch snow, watch the Bills lose another Super Bowl, and watch people you love die of cancer. Once those options are exhausted, there is nothing much left to keep you going, other than drinking or going into recovery. Nothing says fellowship, Buffalo-style, like an Alcoholics Anonymous meeting. If you go to one, say hello to my father for me. He likes to go to a different meeting each morning before work, so as to get the "full flavor" of the Program. For many years, my mother and I have been in Al-Anon, the codependent girl equivalent of AA. We are all used to introducing our friends, sans last names, as "Bob from Wednesday night," or "Louise from Double Winners." Strangely, what with all the snow, drinking, twelve-stepping and cancer that happens in Buffalo, what you cannot do in this town is get someone to speak to you. I know this firsthand.

I have an argument with my father. He explains to me that my mother's brain cancer is a "challenge to his sobriety," and that he can no longer drive me to the hospital to visit her. I ask him who is going to take care of him, when he becomes ill. His answer is, "the state will do that." I tell him communism is no longer the rage. I tell him I think Mario Cuomo is too busy to take time off from work to care for my father. My father tells me I am being cruel, and that he will pray for me.

I hate him. I hate myself. I hate this situation, so I take what I consider to be an understandable course of action: I tell my father, in measured tones over the telephone, that the moment my mother dies, I am going to kill myself. Soon, I begin to panic. The thing is, suicide really does seem as good a plan as any.

Frightened and very much alone, I start dialing. First, I call my friends in New York. All I get are answering machines. It's the week before Christmas, and they are all at parties. I am not embar-

rassed to threaten to kill myself during my mother's terminal illness, but I am, for reasons I might never understand, too ashamed to
call my brothers past midnight, so I don't do that. Finally, swallow-
ing my pride, I look up the Suicide Hotline People in the phone
book, and dial the number. I try to think of how I will even begin
talking about my dying mother and my sobriety-challenged father
to a complete stranger. I wonder if this isn't a story these folks hear
all the time. But there is no need to wonder anything, it turns out.
The phone goes unanswered. It rings. And rings.

Nothing.

I can't believe it. Someone forgot to man the Suicide Hotline
during the holidays. Only in Buffalo. Squatting in the middle of my
mother's bed (in her apartment, for which we continued to pay; it
seemed creepy to give up her place, as she was only fifty-one years
old) wrapped in my mother's expensive down comforter, I sob. I
look like shit. I stink. I have a permanent headache from living off
hospital coffee and Christmas cookies. My brothers and I have
fouled my mother's home: there are candy bar wrappers in the bed,
old magazines, twelve-step literature, laundry in dirty piles on the
floor. And newspapers. Everywhere newspapers, one of which is
the Buffalo weekly arts rag called *Gusto!*

It is impossible to convey to you just how many of these *Gusto!*
things I have had shoved into my bookbag, given to me by well-
meaning Monday-night friends of my mother who insist that I "get
out of the hospital room more often" and "see some theater." "Theresa, Buffalo is really expanding in the arts!" they say. As though I
want to see a fucking play.

In the back of the *Gusto!* are some ads for phone sex services.
They say things like, "One on One with Horny Sluts," and "Live
Talk with Dirty Housewives." I've never called a phone sex service
before. On the other hand, I haven't seriously plotted my suicide
before, either. If I am going to die tonight, I think, I might as well go
out with a bang, so to speak. It's certainly going to be far more
traumatic to my brothers that I want to kill myself, than that I used
my dying mother's credit card to try something new. This is, at
least, my reasoning at the time.

I pick what I think is the sleaziest ad. It is the one with a busty
blonde woman bent over with her ass in the air, her hands on her

nipples, her teeth perfectly straight. "God, she looks in a good mood," I think, and then I dial.

The moment I hear the connection, I clear my throat and announce: "Hello, I have never done this . . ."

But it doesn't matter. What I am hearing is a recording instructing me to "Stay on the Line for the Hottest Talk—" The recording breaks off, and I hear coughing in the background. Coughing?

"Um, hi," I begin, again. "I've never done this before—"

"Wait," a woman's live voice answers. "You are a girl."

"Right," I answer, "I am."

"I don't talk to girls," she says.

Such a night I am having. First, denied my God-given right to call the suicide hotline, and now, rejected by my first phone-sex woman. I am ashamed, and then incensed. I mean, I'm not dialing Alabama. Surely these women have heard every request; mine is *so* different? Besides, no one has asked me what I want! Suddenly, I am feeling very Queer Nation. Right then, I decide to do something unique among Al-Anon members. I stand my ground.

"Can you transfer me?" I ask.

She does. I get transferred to a nicer woman, who sounds more mature. Well, old. But I don't care. I ask her to talk to me about breast-feeding. She decides instead to talk to me about bondage. Whatever. I don't come on the phone, the first time. I do come later, by myself in my mother's bed. For the first time in a long time, I feel alive and beautiful.

It becomes a habit. Phone sex, I mean. I find that I can be stinky, funky, ugly, despairing, with dirty toenails and poor home health care coverage, yet still feel glamorous, sensual, and exciting on the telephone. I start using every break to go downstairs at the hospital and use the phone booths to make nasty calls. Some to women, on my mother's charge card. Some for free to men, on "chat lines." I call after spending the day with my mother, from her apartment, stirring a pot of soup in a ratty bathrobe and bunny slippers, answering the breathy question, "What are you wearing?" with the reply, "Nothing, baby. I am wearing nothing."

Sometimes I am "myself." Sometimes I make up a woman I would like to fuck, someone tall with long dark hair and green eyes, a ballet dancer maybe, and be her on the phone. Whenever anyone asked my name, I would tell them, oh, it's Jane. Jane, to me, stands for Jane Doe. I like the anonymity. Only months later does it occur to me that Jane Doe is a dead person's name.

My father has a way of spinning banality to crystalline perfection. I admit, I am on the dramatic side, but even I was surprised that he could so conveniently forget my threat to commit suicide, and call Christmas morning, suggesting that we go Christmas shopping together. I, characteristically, agreed. We go to the Eastern Hills Mall, where he buys many products for his second wife at Ye Olde Body and Bath Shoppe. Of course, it is snowing. It always snows at this time of year in Buffalo. In the two hours we are at the mall, the snow drifts accumulate up to the door handles on his car.

Now he is nervous. He doesn't want to drive me back to the hospital. He wants me to stay over at his new house, with his new wife, and his new make-believe family that includes a yippy dog. I tell him no. He has to drive me back to the hospital. He then reverses the drama queen business on me, and starts to sob, confessing that AA has taught him he has a crippling fear of driving in the snow. It is his new wife who comes to the rescue, driving me to the hospital, so as not to threaten my father's sobriety.

Momma is sleeping when I get there. She is quiet, snoring a little. The room is blue. The light matches the color of the bruises running up and down my mother's arms from her IVs. I hear the pumps and the drains in time with her breath. She has had her third brain surgery. Her shunt keeps getting infected. Her head is wrapped up in a little turban of white gauze. Her cerebellum is where the tumor was located, so her balance and walking have been taken from her. She ain't going nowhere, she tells me again and again. Even so, she makes the trip to the physical therapy room every day, and tries.

Her eyes open, and they are wet. "Hi. It's me," she says. She often talks like this now, like a child. She asks me to come around to the side of the bed, and I do. I kiss her face, and feel the little whiskers the hormones are causing her to grow. She tells me she wants to show me something. She asks me to hold her arms and pull. She manages to sit up, and I start to cry. "I been doing this for a week, but I told them keep it a secret, it is a Christmas present for Theresa," she says. I cry some more.

She wants me to wheel her down the hall, to look at the Christmas tree. I do, and almost lose control of the wheelchair a few times, which makes us laugh like loons, alone in a deserted secretaries wing of the Cancer Clinic. She was right, the tree is worth the trip. It is tall and high and alone in the snowy field and it has lights on it, and it is perfect. My mom asks me to sing her a song. She always asks me that, and I always say no, which is strange, because I have sung professionally. I say no again, and she says, okay, fine. Can she have some Chinese food?

I call every place in the phone book for Chinese food on Christmas Eve, because my mother is a lunatic, and finally get some people in this dumpy town to feel sorry for me and my crazed dying mother and deliver. Then I dial a number (I have them written in my date book now) and manage some quick phone sex in the downstairs booth. I come, the food comes, and I get on the elevator. When I get upstairs, juggling huge shopping bags full of Chinese food, the first thing I see is my mother sitting in her chair, mouthing my name over and over, silent tears running down her face. I look down at her hand. It has swollen to the size of a softball and is filling up. "I am going to explode," she whispers, her eyes wide.

Yelling, I finally get a nurse, who waddles down to my mother's room, takes a look at her hand, now swollen to the size of a small tetherball, and announces that my mother's line has been "infiltrated." She takes the IV line out of my mother's hand, covers her up with a towel, and begins preparing a fresh needle, muttering to my mother and I about how this line may hurt, the ones in right after the infiltrations always do—

Right then, my mother does a remarkable thing. She looks at the nurse and says,

"Write this down in my chart. No more lines. This is my last Christmas. No more lines."

Clucking in disgust, the nurse does write my mother's demand into her chart and then looks again at the two of us: my mother, IV-less for the first time in a month; me, polluting the room with hundreds of little boxes of greasy Chinese takeout. We eat like dogs. She says she is happy to have the IV out. She is glad to have taken charge of her care, she says. She loves me the best, she says, and she knows she is going to get better soon. She falls asleep before eleven, and I doze in the chair. When I wake up at midnight, and kiss her, I feel something wet and warm running down behind her ear, and I know what it is, because we have gone through this before. It is cerebral spinal fluid. My mother's wrong. There will be more operations, more IVs. She is going to die in this horrible snowy place.

My momma wanted to have one more orgasm before she died. I don't know if she ever thought of masturbating in the hospital room. She was a Catholic schoolgirl at heart. Besides, she was left-handed, and that is where the IVs ran, up her left arm. I hope she took the opportunity on Christmas Eve, when her hand was free, and her hopes were high. I know I did. I took the white down comforter, and went to sleep in the visiting room. There was a tree with blinking lights. Clink, they went. No one else was there; no one else was going to be there. There was a blizzard outside. I used the courtesy telephone to call a phone sex line. I used my mother's charge card to pay for it. I spoke to a woman named Monique (they are all named Monique) and asked her to tell me about her breasts. She started to tell me about bondage. For some reason they all want to give me a bondage story. I asked her to listen instead. Outside the room, I could hear the soft squeak of nurses on late rounds. I took a breath and started slowly, humming at first. The way she used to do it. Then I sang:

> Darling, if you ever go, could I take it? Maybe so.
> Ah, but would I like it? No, not much. . . .

Merry Christmas, Momma.

Boylove

Dorian Key

CIRCLE K

The first time I heard it, it wasn't a shock I guess, sort of like hearing something you knew was coming for a long time even though you're not consciously aware of it, but when it comes it's no big surprise. So when she said it, she whispered but it seemed like a shout, the words so strong I was kinda scared but interested, intrigued, you know? The words so hard, so compelling they couldn't go anywhere but down through my head, down my body they rode, sliding fast until grabbing a hold of my groin like a whole bunch of trouble. And that's what this all is, a whole bunch of trouble, a big box of firecrackers waiting to explode if you just breathe or think wrong. And I was thinking it was a wrong thing, not so good, too dang complicated and you know how I like things all neat and tidy, nice and predictable. But oh, no, this couldn't be that way, could it?

Words can be powerful that way. But even more it was her undertone that made it even worse: sort of dark, sort of taunting. Sort of slow on the uptake I was, at first I thought it was a mistake, a misplaced accusation, unvented rage or something, but then I saw it in her eyes. You know *it,* the thing you're always looking for but don't know what *it* is until it's staring you right in the face, practically running you down like a tanker truck going seventy on a burning, deserted, desert road and you're stuck in place, can't move an inch, can't even think. All you can do is feel, and even though it's feeling mighty wrong in some ways, your heart is telling you it's right, damn right and if you don't lunge at it now, you're probably never going to be that close again, ever. All I could do was stare back like an idiot, and so what did she do? She laughed. Not just a little giggle, but body-shaking hilarity. And then she repeated it, a little louder so everyone in Circle K could hear, but this time with an emphasis on the second word, "You *are* a pedophile, aren't you?"

This cute, young, wicked dyke boy, with a chip as big as that truck on her shoulder, caught you looking a little too long at her. But nothing could really ever be too long with this boy, and nothing could ever be too big, or too dangerous, or too much trouble. So you reached and grabbed that tough shoulder with your dirty, sweaty hand so hard that your knuckles cracked and the sound echoed like a cap blast. Everyone was still staring but they didn't want to mess with freaks like you, so you pulled her out of there with the Sugar Daddy you were going to buy, but instead just stole, in your other hand. You dragged her around the building, slammed her up against the sun-hot concrete wall, shoved the Sugar Daddy in your back pocket, and crushed your mouth to hers and tasted it, sweet, wicked, and hot: boy-dyke spit, tongue, lips, and breath and you couldn't help thinking, it tastes kinda like that sucker in your back pocket, but a whole hell of a lot better. So much fucking better. And you knew you were committed. To loving boys. To being a pedophile. For a long, long while.

ROAD

The last time I saw that boy wasn't the last time, if I have anything to say about it. I'm feeling mighty selfish about the situation, pretty embarrassing for an ethical sap like me, but I've been wanting my way so bad with this that I'm not content to just hang by and do nothing. Usually I would just lecture myself real hard about how I just need to let things unfold, and what is meant to be will happen and all that shit. But I can't sit still with this one 'cause all I want to do is run her down the longest, hottest road we've ever been on. And I'm thinking about all her aspects, not just the sweet boy-curve of her lips, the sinking feeling of her embrace, but also the ragged rush of my heart and lungs when she runs me down, wrestles me rough to that hot blacktop and with her boot presses me down so hard that loose bits of asphalt grind into my cheek and with one last grasping effort my lips open, my tongue sneaks out, and with the great deliberation of a full-mouthed kiss, I taste the road.

LOST BOY

The next thing I know, she throws herself down so that she's sprawled head to toe on top of me and her hand shoves in between us like a hard wooden wedge that wants to push us apart but apparently that's not her intention as she slides her rough, calloused hand, small and powerful into my jeans, under my briefs and grabs my ass like a handhold on a cliff and clutches me hard, digging those fingers into my flesh like thick brutal splinters. My head jerks up from its roadkiss and as my mouth hovers hot and bruised I spit bits of gravel and glass onto the road which glisten like dirty, cheap, fake jewels. Her breath rasps hot and damp on my cheek and she works her lips and teeth like a vise on the back of my neck until I am yowling with pain, frustration, and cheap lust, powerful and dirty. "Unbutton your fucking pants!" she growls. I pause for a moment and she says, "Do it now!" My hand pays good attention as it moves down and pulls open my button-fly. I can't help but grasp my wet cunt and I hold on for life as she yanks my pants and briefs down over my ass. I feel the accompanying pull of her jeans and the hard jut of her dick between my bare asscheeks and as she forces her way into my ass, I cry with the vulnerability of a love-starved, lost boy. She works her way in and out of me with careful patience until she can't control herself any longer and is pounding into me and we are sliding down that rough, ragged road on a furious gritty ride, her cock up my ass, and my hand in my cunt. As she finishes me off, I lift my tear-stained face from the hot, dusty pavement and pant, ragged and hard, "Now you tell me who's the fucking pedophile." Her kiss, deep and biting, is the only answer I need.

Pumping Iron, Pumping Cocks:
Sex at the Gym

Lawrence Schimel

Tonight I held another man's cock in my hands as he played with his nipples. I hadn't meant to engage in any sort of sex this evening, and in many ways the encounter doesn't qualify as sex, per se, at least not on my part. It would be wrong to say that sex happened to me. I aided and abetted sex, but I did not have sex.

I'd gone to the gym, and after my workout had gone to relax in the heat of the steam room. It wasn't very hot, the steam having begun to dissipate. I stared around me, deliberated where to sit among the half-dozen men on the benches. I work out at the Chelsea Gym in New York, an all-male, almost all-queer gym notorious for its frisky steam rooms. Often, I've had to deal with grab-first-ask-later queens, attracted by my youth (as if youth alone equaled beauty).

I took a vacant corner spot, and pretty much ignored my companions. Two of them separately stared at me intently as they stroked their groins, and I acknowledged that I was aware of their hungry intentions and disinterested. All heads turned whenever the door opened, and I too looked up at each newcomer, each new naked body—and also scowled at the rush of cold air they brought with them. The steam evaporated further. We waited. The spaces on the benches filled up. Men shifted to allow a newcomer to sit. A nice-looking, well-hung man took the empty seat next to me. At last, the jets kicked in, and the room filled with vapor. I closed my eyes, rubbed my tired muscles as the waves of heat washed over me, easing tension.

When I looked up again, all of the other men in the steam room had paired off, their hands in one another's laps as they jerked each other off. The man next to me and I were the only two who weren't partaking, though his dick was hard and he'd been stroking it since this furtive sexual activity began. I found him the most attractive man in the room. I think objectively he'd probably be the most attractive man in the room. He had a nicely defined body, a cock with enough heft to it—he was the biggest of any of us without getting into obscene or unmanageable sizes.

The pairs around us continued their motions, arms flexing. He fixed me with a look.

So, I gave him a helping hand.

Now, I can engage in sex without having an erection, I've done so before, and can have a very enjoyable time. I can get fucked without having an erection, and have an enjoyable time of it. I can suck someone off without myself getting an erection, and again enjoy myself immensely.

Tonight, however, as I am holding this man's cock in my hands and stroking him, I am hardly present in the act. I am in a private space, inside my body. I go to the gym to get out of my head. As a writer, I spend all day in my head, cerebrally, thinking, engaging the blank page, creating narrative, whether fiction, poetry, or essay like what you're reading now.

He's got a very nice cock that I'd like to play with again under other circumstances. But right now, it's not very meaningful. I'm tired, my body aches, I'm feeling not in the least erotic. I'd like someone to give me a massage, to feed me, and perhaps to hold me while I fall asleep. I'm not aroused and I'm not taking any pleasure out of jerking him off. Why then am I doing it?

Because he's attractive. Because I'm curious. Because I feel I should be responding to him, the situation.

Because I know I'll write this essay when I get home.

I've never fooled around before in the steam room, even though I've watched others do so many times. I like being in the presence of sex, even without any intention of taking part. Sometimes, if there's an attractive man in the showers with me, I'll hope he comes into the steam room after me and fools around with someone. Sometimes, later, in the privacy of my bed, I'll remember the look of him reaching over to fist his neighbor's cock with one hand and his own in the other. I'll remember and jerk off, at last giving myself permission to be turned on.

I'm never aroused while I'm there, watching.

For me, the gym has a nonerotic boundary around it. I come to the gym with an editor of mine—my workout partner—and so right away I am nervous about propriety. Sure, he's a gay man, and has probably had sex in similar situations himself. But the idea of him coming into the steam room while I'm engaged in some sexual act causes embarrassment and shame in me. What is meant to be anonymous sex—quite different from sex engaged under other circumstances—is no longer anonymous. There is a confusion of boundaries between the chaste, almost-asexual (although politically sexual, that is, with a political sexuality) professional persona and the private, erotic, uninhibited sexual self.

The steam room of the gym is not a space designated for sex. Had I run into an editor—or anyone else I knew—at a sexclub, a space designated for sex, I would not feel embarrassment or shame. I might be nonplussed, perhaps perturbed at having to interact with someone I am unprepared to deal with, the way I begrudge running into certain acquaintances on the street and having to do the dance of pleasantries. But shame, when we were both obviously there for the same reason, and that reason was sex?

Tonight I am flirting with this taboo, with this fear of being discovered engaged in sex, that adolescent thrill of sneaking a parent's or older sibling's or friend's pornography to jerk off to.

A lot of people I know from the outside world come to this gym. And, since I spend so much time at home, alone, working in solitude, these daily gym excursions have begun to provide me with a social network of casual acquaintance, people who are familiar, with whom I sometimes gossip. They are my equivalent of office friendships, and our relationships are casual—and nonerotic. Any of these people—there were a handful of them upstairs while I was working out—might come into the steam room at any moment.

Can I get off without getting caught? But part of me wants to get caught. I am part of a community, and this stud I'm playing with is like a Trophy Fuck: whether it's enjoyable or not, you take him home because everyone else wants him, and it improves your social standing to have bedded him. I want to be caught because I want the attention. And I want the attention now, not what I know I'll get from writing about this experience later tonight in this essay.

I want to be caught because some part of me wonders why my dick isn't hard, won't get hard, even now that I've decided to play with this man next to me, and I am trying to prove something to myself about my identity as a gay man, according to a set of arbitrary and amorphous, undefined external social rules about what it means to be gay. In the "straight" locker room in high school, I'd be embarrassed to have a woody while looking at another guy, but in queer locker room bravado, I'm embarrassed not to have one—especially doing what I'm doing. If we were in one of our apartments, I'd be unconcerned by all this social pressure and anxiety about acquaintances interrupting us, and would therefore have an erection. I'd like to be in one of our apartments, where the acts we'd allow ourselves would be more extensive and enjoyable.

In the steam room, there is no such thing as foreplay. It is all speed, all animal sex. Men do not kiss in the steam room. Sex, for me, is less fun without kissing. Men do not really caress, not for the pleasure of rubbing bodies against each other, the intimacy of skin. One man might run his hand over another's thigh, but it is with hopeful inquisitiveness, or with the intent to get his neighbor aroused already so they can get off before someone comes in.

Anyone entering the room breaks up any and all action. Everyone freezes like rabbits caught in headlights. Hands drop whatever they're holding and cover crotches, trying to hide the erections that (hopefully) are too long to fit behind a palm.

It's curious to me, how these men will have sex in a public space—the gym—and yet are so self-conscious the moment they're reminded of the public nature of it, in the scrutiny of a stranger. This prudishness is somewhat practical: sexual activity in the gym is forbidden by the city's Health Department and thereby the gym's management. Memberships could be revoked if someone who works at the gym found them engaged in sex and reported it, or if other members complained. But the truth of the matter is, most of the guys who work at the gym don't care one way or the other, and the other members of the gym usually crowd around to watch whenever sex happens in the steam room, hoping they might join in, like a backroom frenzy.

The difference between these steam-room jerk-offs—or the more rare suck-offs—and those of a backroom, however, lies in the nature of the space. The gym is not an arena intended for sex. It is not supposed to be happening there, and everyone is aware of this fact. When two (or more) men in the steam room begin to engage in sex, they are implicitly asking for the consent of everyone else in the room. Onlookers might not vocalize their consent for this activity to take place—although, alas, too often sex is egged on by onlookers whose sexuality is limited to lame and simplistic porno movie dialogue—but they have not withheld their consent either.

A newcomer has not yet had a chance to withhold his dissent, so everything comes crashing to a stop while everyone takes stock of each other and evaluates what is going on and how they should react. Surreptitiously, hands crawl back into neighbors' crotches, and the newcomer either watches, takes part, or ignores what's going on.

In the steam room around us, men continued jerking each other off in pairs. The man whose cock I held lost interest in my playing with him, because I had so little interest in it. Because he could not reciprocate. My lack of arousal disturbed him. Perhaps insulted him, in the rules of queer locker room bravado. I should've been hard and horny, I should've been wanting him. I had a curiosity, nothing more. He shifted away from me. I let his cock fall from my hands, graciously stopping. He stood up, and left the steam room. The pairs of men around us paused as the door opened—the glare of headlights—but then resumed.

I was disappointed. I felt embarrassed, among these other men who were involved in their own pleasure. Because I did not finish off the guy I was playing with, the implication is that I was not doing a good job. I felt a twinge of shame: If I had given him more pleasure, he would have stayed until he came. If I'd been hard, he would've stayed until he came. I failed at sex.

But these thoughts evaporated, and most of my shame with it. I still felt that irrational social peer pressure, that I should've been aroused despite my anxiety surrounding my professional life. But I know that judging my "performance" was irrelevant to what passed between us. Things weren't clicking. We engaged in sexual activity because we were seated next to each other, not out of any desire for each other. I was not interested in having sex, but was engaging in it to ask myself an intellectual question: How far would this man let me go with him? And also: How far was I willing to go with him, in this situation?

But having proposed these questions and being in the moment with the answer, I was surprised to discover the answer—a frisson like being confronted with a newcomer's scrutiny.

I returned into myself. I glanced at the men around me, as they built toward the grunting, messy climax of sex. My disinterest returned. The steam was dissipating again, the door was slightly ajar. I stood up; I left the steam room. The guy I was playing with was not in the showers. I saw him through the window as I passed the sauna.

I showered, left.

I wrote this essay. Alone, in my apartment, I thought about the scenario again—the feel of his cock in my hands, his initial eagerness as he twists a nipple as I work him, the thrill of doing this in public, my eagerness to be caught—and I was hard.

Under My Skin

Ron Athey

MI BARRIO LOCO

Through the many changes I've been through in my life, there has only been one constant: tattooing. I think the tattoos started off as a purely sexual turn-on for me. On the south side of Pomona—a Chicano barrio outside of Los Angeles where I grew up—they were the only status symbol besides driving a '54 Chevy. Back then, I was a *mariqita* (prissy little faggot) with blond hair and blue eyes, and the nastiest young *vatos* used to fight about whose house I went to after school. There I was, a little blondie chug-a-lugging on numerous penises of the neighborhood gangster-trainees, becoming more and more obsessed with the tattoos of their older brothers. Most of the tattoos were done in jail with a cassette motor and guitar string setup, they were impressive fine-lined illustrations of sacred hearts, crosses, women with big hair, peacocks, and guns.

THE WEARING OF THE TURBAN

A few years later, I hooked up with my first real boyfriend, Rudy. I guess he wasn't really my boyfriend, because he lived with a woman, but he was mine during the day, when she was at work. He had just served a nine-year sentence in the penitentiary for God-knows-what, when I met him. He didn't seem to want to tell me, so I probably accurately fantasized that it was a gang murder. Rudy played a lot of mind-fuck games with me, like making me wear a towel around my head so I looked like I had long hair (this is the famous "wearing of the turban," an honor for cocksuckers in jail). I found this glamour girl parody he was involving me in particularly degrading as I had recently discovered punk rock and was into my black-dyed, short-cropped hairstyle, but the lower I sank for him, the more turned on I got.

He would fuck my teenaged ass, then make me clean his cock off with my mouth. Life with Rudy terrified me, but at the same time I came to worship him for turning me out, bringing me into another world far away from my family. This life consisted of violent sex and intense role-playing, where I was in real danger of having my face smashed in if I did the wrong thing. Unfortunately, it also included shooting dope and hustling money. He showed me how to steal car batteries and where to sell them. After three or four months of this lifestyle, I began to wonder if I was going to get out alive.

On my last weekend with Rudy, I commemorated the end with a tattoo. I took thread and wrapped it around the tip of a sewing needle, and dipped it in India ink. I tattooed a teardrop in my right eye to match his. I knew by Chicano gang codes, this meant I had either done five years in the pen, or had killed someone, but I loved Rudy's tear so much I was willing to live with the stigma. Seven years later, after kicking a heroin, methadone, and Valium habit, I tattooed a red tear under the black one, to dramatically mark my deliverance.

PUNK ROCK DUDE

Being a heroin addict with a tattooed face went a long way in the punk scene, 1980. I met Rozz Williams, founder of the Goth band Christian Death, and soon thereafter my second boyfriend. He pierced my nipple with a safety pin and I tattooed his name on my wrist. Later, I went from tattoo shop to tattoo shop with a hundred dollar bill in my pocket, looking for someone to tattoo a black widow spider on my forehead. It took a few tries to find someone who would do it. There was a certain amount of stigma around tattooing at the time. It has traditionally been a lower class and underworld practice in the United States, mostly bikers and military men.

Tattooing the face is seen as much more extreme, only seen on ex-cons, skinheads, and the occasional sideshow oddity. Even though I crossed that line and had my face tattooed seven different times, I always dissuaded other friends from getting their faces tattooed. "You won't be able to handle it," I'd say. "Who do you think you are, me?"

Around this time, I was obsessed with Edward, the singer of Nervous Gender (originators of the techno/homo/punk scene), and we eventually became fuck buddies. We decided our first tattoo together had to be our motto—infinite pain and suffering. Edward designed a crown of thorns in the shape of the infinity symbol, which we both got tattooed on our wrists. The clincher was that I had to show my undying love and affection, and tattooed his name on the back of my neck. In 99 percent of all cases, this means the end.

MODPRIM™

In 1981, I gained access to *LOVE* magazine, a brilliant magazine published in Italy by Annie Sprinkle. In it, there were pregnant women in bondage, essays on sex and avant garde, and most important to my life and development, a huge spread on Fakir Musafar. Fakir coined the phrase Modern Primitives to describe Western peoples drawn to ancient cultures and rituals, most of whom express this through tribal tattoos and piercings. MODPRIM™, as it has sarcastically become known, was a movement of sorts, that became overexposed by the media and parodied by the mainstream, before it had a chance to really exist. Perhaps that was the nature of it, but I had hoped it would stay exclusive: hardcore and sexy. Instead it became a dorkfest of sorts, and in some factions quite hippy dippy.

In the early 1980s when tribal tattoo enthusiasts Leo Zulueta and Dan Thome came to L.A., from San Francisco and Guam, respectively, they found a few willing subjects like myself, ready to be heavily tattooed in the black islander style. Thome was a merchant sailor, and sailed around the Pacific, learning hand tattooing from Samoans, and collecting patterns from Micronesian islands. I was going to get heavily tattooed no matter what, and feel fortunate I found this neotribal style before I got too much crap Americana coverage. I really connected with the bold "see it from a block away" graphics of the South Pacific style. It really suited me, and at the time, it seemed like a few of us were reinventing ourselves, though most people didn't get the design value of thick black patches and just thought they were cover-ups.

THE ROUGH AND ROCKY ROAD MAP

Historically, very few men have had their entire bodies tattooed in one week. Most tattoo enthusiasts have mapped their bodies with different styles by several artists, for a variety of important occasions: camaraderie, love, death, transition. The Army, Navy, or Marines. My body can be construed as a map, if you can figure out the order. While tribal designs take the most space, the purity is occasionally broken with a meaningful totem. I dream about tattoos, read magazines, look through research books. I've spent years going to tattoo conventions, talking to people on the street, and hanging out in tattoo shops. This is an immense obsession, which, like most fetishes, is incomprehensible to those not involved.

All right, I've had a few tattoos covered—"Rozz," "Edward," and a few botched amateur hand-done jobs—but it's taken seventeen years to cover my body this much, and frankly, I may as well have been born this way. When I had my first shop tattoo—the spider on my forehead—the tattooist said, "Don't get this unless you want to talk about tattoos for the rest of your life."

I had no idea how true those words were. The most common, annoying response is, "Oooh, did that hurt?" I hear it one to a hundred times a day. Perhaps the second most-asked question is, "What if you get tired of it when you get older?" This intimates a judgment, that this random person on the street feels you have made a mistake. And that they're owed an answer, because you have made yourself stand out. I say, "Older than thirty-four years old? Do you think when I'm sixty, that I'll wake up one morning and look at myself in the mirror and suddenly realize that my life's been all wrong?" It's hard for a nontattooed person to understand the feeling that you might as well have been born with the pattern you chose, imperfections and all. To suddenly reject your tattoos is to reject the history it has come to represent. For all of my adult life, that telling tattoo ink has gotten under my skin.

TATTOO MAP

1. Left hand: cross, star, spider; skull and crossbones, bat, "Rozz" (all done by hand, though pieces done on wrist are now covered in a solid black cuff); black widow spider, web, Borneo hand patterns, waves and stars on knuckles
2. Right hand: waves; mystic knot; infinite crown of thorns; Egyptian eye (covered with tribal linework); Hawaiian-inspired triangle checks
3. Arms: Marquesan stripes, skulls with daggers, Tibetan fire (only color);
4. Chest: Maori woodcutting patterns, Hawaiian pattern, sacred heart, mythical Japanese water lizards
5. Ribcage: Maori wood-carving designs—unfinished
6. Upper back: Iban funeral altar pattern; lower back: assorted Japanese arrows, fleur-de-lis-esque pattern
7. Head, back of neck: Tibetan swastika, EDWARD (covered with black triangles); face and right side of head: black widow spider, crown of thorns, cross, black tear, red tear; throat: traditional Borneo throat piece
8. Buttocks: spirals taken from Tibetan banner
9. Outer thighs: Marquesan patterns mimicking arms; inner: Samoan/Americana bastardization
10. Shin: bulldagger (honor given to me by butch girl bikers)
11. Abdomen: skull (done single-needle), neotribal gridwork; pubis has the name CHRIST because it fit.

Captured Downstream: The Backsplash from Urinal Screen Marketing

Michael Scarce

While working as the Coordinator of Ohio State University's Rape Education and Prevention Program in 1996, I launched a rape-awareness campaign with the intent of targeting a male audience and broadening discussions of rape and sexuality in the surrounding community. Rather than fashion a tired bumper sticker, poster, or button, I decided to custom-print hundreds of urinal screens with the slogan, "You hold the power to stop rape in your hand" and deposit them in men's urinals across campus. Urinal screens, for those unfamiliar with such gender-specific janitorial supplies, are flat pieces of rubber with small holes. The screens serve three main purposes: they prevent the urinal drain from clogging with debris such as cigarettes and paper towels; they are usually scented and help to deodorize the urinal; and their strategic design helps to prevent urine stream backsplash.

So why not add a fourth preventive function to this male device? They seemed like the perfect site for community dialogue about men's responsibility for preventing sexual assault. Urinal screens are inexpensive; the low-end models cost less than two dollars each. They have a life of approximately six months (much longer than a newspaper ad or billboard) and their audience is somewhat discouraged from touching, let alone vandalizing them once they're in place. I anticipated the notoriety of the campaign would reach far more people than the men who actually saw the screens, increasing the effectiveness of the project in terms of sheer numbers.

Intentionally matching the message with the medium in this particular social marketing campaign represents a deeper duality of complex contradictions. Rape is considered a grim topic of serious,

adult concern, yet the slogan carries a less-than-subtle pun of immature bathroom humor. Restrooms and sexual violence are highly
privatized, yet simultaneously public phenomena, both individual
and communal in nature. In addition, male acts of urination and
rape both typically involve a penis. Despite cultural emphasis on
the penis as a "sexual" part of male anatomy, excretion and violence
are not always defined as sexual acts. But some people do not
dichotomize rape with sex, and for some, urination in the form of
watersports is a sexual act. These competing definitions and con-
notations quickly became apparent when contentious responses to
the urinal screen campaign began streaming into my office.

BACKSPLASH

Three different janitorial supply companies refused to print the
screens, solely on the basis of the textual message, causing a two-
month delay with the project. The first janitorial supply company
initially agreed to print the screens. A week later, however, they
called to reject our business. Apparently the company was a small,
family-owned business. The man who took the order found the
project humorous and interesting. However, his wife and daughter,
who worked in the company as administrative assistants, put their
foot down and forced him to rescind his agreement to fill the order.
He relayed to us that they were concerned their products would be
used "by some radical women's group on campus." The second
janitorial company rejected the sale on the basis of the slogan, but
refused to comment further. A third company, like the first, also
initially agreed to print the screens, so we sent them the textual
artwork immediately. Within a few days of receiving the order, the
notoriety of the slogan had sparked a great deal of discussion
among the company's office staff members. Such heated debates on
sexual assault and gender issues ensued that the company contacted
us to reject the sale purely in the interest of eliminating the increasing tension and internal conflict it had caused among their em-
ployees. After this third failure, I purchased five hundred blank
urinal screens from yet another supply company, found a local
industrial printer who was willing and able to do the job, and received the final product a week later.

After sending out a brief press release, I delivered the urinal screens to the folks at Ohio State University's Department of Physical Facilities. Nate Taylor, the wonderful man in charge of the department, saw to it that custodians installed them in the most highly trafficked classroom buildings across campus. About the same time, I began receiving calls from reporters who wanted interviews about the campaign. In addition to local television, radio, and print media, the project garnered attention from *USA Today, Newsweek, Playboy,* BBC Radio in London, the *Rush Limbaugh* television show, and *The Tonight Show with Jay Leno*. Surprisingly, Limbaugh found the project humorous and spoke of it in a positive light. He discovered the screens in *USA Today*, read the slogan on his show, and burst into a fit of laughter. Soon thereafter, he grew serious and commented how sad our society must be that we actually have to tell men not to rape. (Rush's approval sent a chill up my spine, but made a great addition to my video scrapbook.)

In the weeks following the implementation of the campaign, I collected a multitude of written responses from concerned citizens expressing their opinions on the matter. Ranging from compliments to complaints, I was especially appreciative of those who offered constructive criticisms. More than one university professor noted the slogan's poor grammar and suggested the revision "You hold in your hand the power to stop rape" to convey that power, rather than rape, resides in the hand. I assured them I would make a correction if I ever commissioned a second edition. One inventive undergraduate student suggested that I should have printed the screens with a special pH-sensitive ink so the text would only appear in the presence of an acidic substance. Another student discovered the flat rubber screens made great Frisbees.

I was amazed by the range of interpretations that people read into the slogan. In a letter to the editor of our campus newspaper, student Blair King wrote, "If [they] continue placing these urinal screens, they run the risk of reinforcing rather than challenging the idea that rape is about sex."[1] Huh? If a reference to the penis was the problem, I think we ran more of a risk of equating urination with rape. For example, if I beat someone in the head with a rolling pin, you wouldn't call it baking. The whole point of the urination theme was to challenge men to think about their penises in nonsexual ways, such as a tool for excretion or a weapon with which they may choose to violate others.

In a letter to the editor of the *Columbus Dispatch,* concerned citizen Thomas Meehan proclaimed, "This message not only won't stop rape, but it also trivializes a serious problem. This is not a genuine effort toward a meaningful solution. It is little more than a fraternity house wisecrack."[2] Mr. Meehan seemed to think I was under the delusion that the campaign would, in and of itself, prevent all rape on campus. These kinds of criticisms ignore the difference between awareness and prevention, two public health strategies that do not always overlap. As for my trivialization of rape, I found most of the complainants to be seriously out of touch with the average male college student. Messages that brim with doom and despair have little impact on changing the behavior of these men. If scare tactics do not deter underage drinking, smoking, and unsafe sex, why would they work for sexual assault? Humor can be an appropriate and powerful tool to affect audiences in ways other forms of outreach cannot.

On Q-Study, the academic queer studies e-mail discussion list, Richard Herrell responded, "Arranging for people to piss on a message is not likely a way to encourage a thoughtful response." The idea that urinating on something is a form of degradation and defilement clearly comes from those who do not enjoy watersports. Even if men symbolically piss on my piece of work as an act of hostility, this indicates they have read the slogan and personalized it to some degree, which I consider a splashing success.

The invasion of an all-male space by a message obviously and anatomically targeting men came across as something of a threat to many men on campus. Student William Pees (yes, that really is his last name) complained, "As a man, I don't look forward to being accused of rape every time I use a public restroom on campus. And I resent the trivialization of rape that redefining 'rapist' as 'anyone who uses a urinal' constitutes."[3] Perhaps a bit sensitive to issues related to his namesake, Pees clearly believed a message tailored for a specific audience was all-accusatory male bashing. One anonymous man called my office to complain that he shouldn't "have" to look at things that make him uncomfortable. Instead of recommending he use a stall (which could disturb him further by forcing him to sit down to pee), I suggested that we all have uncomfortable encounters that violate our visual senses. For example, I find suburban nuclear families in sport utility vehicles quite distressing, but I do not seek legislation banning them from public sight (at least not yet). One man challenged me to create a parallel campaign for women's restrooms. I informed him that, given the urinal screen controversy, I was sure the university administration would not approve my other idea—self-defense tips for women on custom-printed Sani-Bags.

My favorite complaint came from a letter to the university president. Joseph Baehr suggested, "Do not be surprised if one of the less sober, less intelligent, less concerned males decides to use that power to rape his girlfriend. Remember, the thought may not have been there until you gave it to him!" Yeah, right, and safer sex education increases teen pregnancy, needle exchange programs increase drug use, and a woman's right to choose inspires casual third trimester abortions. I cannot believe a ten-word sentence would generate a "Eureka!" from men who have never considered, exercised, or benefited from their male privilege—chiefly because these men do not exist. If I had that kind of omnipotence with my writing, I would not be working in the low-pay field of rape prevention.

There were many positive responses as well, although generally less entertaining. An e-mail from profeminist author and activist John Stoltenberg said, "The urinal action idea is inspired. I hope it gets copied all over the country." While flattered, I could not help but wonder how both Limbaugh and Stoltenberg, Andrea Dworkin's radical comrade, could both agree on anything related to sexual politics.

The various responses were all situated within a larger dialogue about the complexity of rape, sexuality, and the cultural meanings embedded in gendered human bodies. These discussions, generated by the screens and the media coverage surrounding them, would not have otherwise taken place in many cases. Reaching millions of people, the campaign propelled "taboo" and "inappropriate" sexual topics from the realms of private into public, then back into private, and so on. This circularity produced a dissemination of sexuality into culture that I find transgressive, productive, and intensely pleasurable. In fact, I continue to pack urinal screens in my luggage whenever I travel, leaving them in the men's rooms of restaurants, bars, hotels, and tourist attractions around the world.

NOTES

1. King, Blair. Letter to the Editor, *The Lantern* (OSU newspaper), May 20, 1996, p. 5

2. Meehan, Thomas. Letter to the Editor, *Columbus Dispatch,* May 28, 1996, p. A6.

3. Pees, William. Letter to the Editor, *The Lantern,* May 20, 1996, p. 5.

Slipping

Jennifer Natalya Fink

1978—UPSTATE NEW YORK:
SUNDAY SCHOOL

Can women rape men? The smell of bacon sizzling fills the air of the campus student union where the Ithaca Association of Jewish Studies holds its earnest Sunday afternoon youth education seminars. Tanya refuses to call it Sunday school; despite the bacon and the hippie teachers she insists on *shul*, demands to be in the class with the older kids because the guy who does real Talmud and modern Hebrew, who cracks jokes about reform Jews with their organ players and ecumenical English prayers—Judaism lite, Christianity without Christ—Mike someone, with thick black sideburns, not a rabbi but a true rebbe teacher, PhD in maybe Yiddish; Mike does older kids only.

"This week we'll talk about women's liberation, Rashi, and Isaiah 3:1. I think," he says with a smile not quite at her, "that what Rashi really means here is, can women rape men?"

1979—UPSTATE NEW YORK:
TRAINING FOR THE BAT MITZVAH

Can women rape men? In the morning before shul, in the room her mother decorated in yellow checkers, Tanya's fingers repeat the wet questions, angering the furry sides, picturing the section of the Talmud black bold-faced questions blunt across the page: if your neighbor is retiling his roof and it is hot so he gets naked then slips (perhaps his feet are sweaty because of the heat), and below him she is lying on her back on a yellow checkered picnic blanket (also naked because of the heat), and he slips, his sweaty body falling over her her hand rubbing fast reddening her face boiling up under the yellow and white comforter who, yes, who is liable if he falls onto her, penetrates her quite by accident, their sweat mingling only for a minute but the damage is done. Unintentional but because of the heat he slipped, she's raped, damaged; who is liable her hand grabbing for the answer as she comes it flashes in black and white like as newspaper headline: Can women rape men?

All night Mike dreams of fucking Josh. Coming on his sweet undead face, some form of frontal intercourse that does not involve penetration, really. It's like fucking Malka all the familiar positions just with Josh's smile, Josh's short, thick body where Malka would be squeezing out against the sheets, but Mike just awakens hard and confused running to piss in the bathroom that smells like her deodorant. The first fuck Josh dream since his death.

Basically, you talk. It begins with a series of questions. "So what does this week's portion tell us?" Before your coat is off, before he leads you to the little windowless study between the bedroom with the ancient lace coverlet and the metallic bathroom, before you dissect the portion or learn some bit of ritual or history or Hebrew, you talk. And answer. Even in the subzero chill factor Upstate winters with their endless student suicides, Mike Silverstein always seemed to be sweating. Sweating and talking: the words pushing moisture through his black hair, soaking his kipah, his mustache. Tanya has never seen a mustache as black and thick as his. They start at four on Sundays and Wednesdays and talk Torah until one of her parents remembers to pick her up at seven or eight. They hate all the driving but figure two shots of hippie Jewdom a week will inoculate her against Christmas trees and local boys with bad teeth and snowmobiles. The only drop of Torah, mishnah, and gmorah she will remember is one minor portion regarding Jewish law's stance on the ethical and legal repercussions of putting glass on your fence. To keep your sheep in. And your neighbor is injured. Also that there are fifteen different interpretations from the mystical to the legal and back again.

Can women rape men?

In today's portion there are seven commentaries on liability in sexual matters. There is sweat dripping beneath his scalp, threading along his black hair and mustache. Even though injured virgins and glass on fences may not seem relevant, each commentary tries to interpret it in relation to larger social issues. He is looking past her serious nodding head toward the window above her chair. Josh's chest sweaty against his. The room soundless. Their chests glued together, everything heavy and wet. He cannot remember a single mole on that chest though he suspects there were many. Only the sweat, the sweat stinking into the sheets the next morning, every morning. He knows every note of its scent.

"Can women rape men?" he asks as they talk past the time when her mother's battered red Volkswagen with its peeling "Pollution Stinks" sticker should whisk her out of his driveway past Talmudic debate toward a fresh salad served up on the good oak table in the orange shag living room. Daylight has passed and the study is dark—and perhaps if there were like ten women and one guy, or a girl with a gun and one guy—she can't see his features or his thick black mustache—and the mechanics are fuzzy: a group of tall blonde women driving up leaping out, tackling him down, knocking his kipah off, dozens of long red nails ripping his black hair from the scalp as they pull down his pants—then the mechanics fuzz up the frame. "But you can't *make* him hard," he says under his breath and yeah she nods, like she knows this, the disappointment washing through her. She suddenly feels the want, the fierce want for women to be able to rape men. On principle. "I mean, you can't *force* him to shoot," he says louder. She misses the way he's watching her, doesn't catch the way his mouth is hanging in waiting, remember-ing Josh's eyes squinting closed as he is fucked solid. He has a habit, she has noticed, of stroking the hairs on his left forearm with his right hand when he concentrates. "No," she talks as he strokes it, "no I guess not quite rape then, but they could take him by force up his asshole or something, right?"

A man is shingling a roof and it is hot so he gets naked. On the grass beneath him, a woman is also getting hot and gets naked, and he slips and falls on her, and she is slippery from the Hawaiian Tropic Extra Dark Coconut tanning oil and he slips right in and she wants damages. Can she collect? What if she were on the roof, sweaty and shingled, and he were oiled up and waiting below? "The Talmud is quite specific on this," he tells her as the red Volkswagen drives up. "Read it for next time and tell me how you think this applies today. I'll give you a hint," he winks as she walks toward the car, "it has something to do with the fundamental difference between Christianity and Judaism."

It is a peeing contest that doesn't end. Poised as far from the bowl as they could get, rated on arc as well as distance. Josh is the messy one, splattering on the white tile, aim off from his inevitable giggling. Malka turns toward him in her sleep, curled around herself. They sneak the usual glances down, yes, but it's actually their pee arching over, intersecting above the bowl, that fascinates Mike. An elaborate Olympic-style ratings system is developed that he tries to recall during the funeral but it is the details of the arc that he remembers instead: Mike's perfect curve intersecting Josh's wiggling line. Inside Malka, her body all wet and muscle, he rocks back there, watching the funeral, watching what is no longer Josh disappear.

She is watching *Charlie's Angels* jiggle toward the camera, asking herself the question she will ask all future lovers: which Angel do you like the best? There is Farrah who everyone likes, fair like the blind scales of justice they teach you in social studies. She smiles back at Farrah as she reaches for the chips. Or Kelly, almost boyish, almost bright. She never chooses Kelly. Then there's Sabrina, also the name of Sabrina the Teenage Witch on Saturday morning cartoons. Like the witch, Sabrina is the brunette. Sabrina's red lipstick and archèd eyebrows smirk into the camera hinting at something too rank for prime time. A husky bit of air whistles between her perfect teeth before each predictable line. Oh, Charlie! Really! I'd never! Charlie's Angels never see Charlie, who directs them to knock out the bad guys while knocking back a frosty drink between the bosoms of two bikinis.

"The difference between Judaism and Christianity," it turns out, "is that for Christians sin is a kind of, well, existential state." His hand waves to underscore *state* his lips curling a bit as she sits across from him beneath the window watching, watching. "Whereas it is one's conscious *will*, one's choices and intentions, not the mere fact of being human that are sinful in Judaism. A man tiling a roof slips and falls into a quick rape but did not intend it, did not think of it so while he is economically liable for damages he is not *morally* liable; he has broken something rather than sinned against it," says Rabbi Akiba. Asleep but for a hand cupping his balls, softly first then too hard. She likes to wake him before the alarm already perfumed and lipsticked. Perfectly put together he always thinks as he rolls onto her still asleep but for the hand. And hours later he shifts in his chair remembering the hand too hard watching this child pull her long mousy hairs into her mouth sucking their ends desperate to understand two types of liability. Always a little desperate to learn.

Sabrina could be a Jew. With those intentional eyebrows, that sucking noise aiming to undercut Farrah's giggles. Definite Jew.

1979—MANCHESTER, ENGLAND

She is not permitted to hear him. See him, yes: talking and moving inside the grainy screen like any other paunchy earnest public figure. But where at home *fuck* and *shit* would be dubbed out, here his whole voice, not his words or his "free speech," but his voice cannot ever be heard. His mouth chews up words fast, but by British Broadcasting Regulation a voice with a mild lilt is dubbed in unsynchronized with his quick mouth. She watches it moving and stopping and after the stranger's voice. In the beginning there was darkness. Hear oh Israel the Lord is God the Lord is One. His voice is two. The state-supplied voice heard and the unhearable One. She watches him after school each day on the news, wondering how they chose this rather calming voice: did they audition hundreds of northern Irish middle-aged Catholic actors, roomfuls of Jerry Sand look-alikes practicing militant Republican speeches in the corners of the TV station's office, waiting their turn patiently as Jerry never would? Does this voice "actually" approximate Jerry's or is it precisely a certain quantity of difference from Jerry's they're after? Or is it this dissolving, this sliding away from content that this dubbing produces, which the censors demand? His voice, not his words censored.

God's voice is unhearable. Unbearable. God demanded Abraham sacrifice his son, not like the other gods in town who need blood to make new men, who need blood to produce their much-vaunted love, no our God cruel God doesn't *need* this sacrifice. There is no reason for it. Except for the senseless, unreasonable desire to see

Abraham's willingness to kill his son for no reason. Nowadays, the Book dubs God, appears in his place, where His voice would be. God is silent now. At school they get new notebooks with greenish pages lined with blue.

Dear Mike:
    Here in Manchester it is even rainier than in Ithaca and the Jews here even the atheists all live together & go to school together (me included!). We wear uniforms recite prayers before lunch and get tons of homework. Everyone still calls me "The Yank" but it's OK I've got a few friends now. Hey Mike, if the difference between Judaism and Christianity is that Jews have to do something bad to be bad, not just think about it, then I think a woman can only rape a man if she's a Christian. You see? So wow, if you rape a man you turn into a Christian ha ha. But here's a tricky one: suppose I want to rape men but I know it's impossible? I fully intend to carry out the act, but the mechanics slip me up. So then I'm maybe a Buddhist, right?

In the dream, Josh is between the walls. Inside them, walking from room to room as Mike teaches and sleeps and fucks through his day. Something happens, maybe Dead Josh talks, but he cannot remember it now. Lisa and Amy and Renee are on the couch, practicing his new arrangement for L'chah Dodee, oh we greet you Sabbath Queen. They make each record in one day, that's the rule: Friday mornings, he writes the arrangement and sets up the equipment. He takes students until four, then the girls show up, rehearse, and then bang they record. However tanked up with pizza and giggles they start out, by the time their voices are cutting into the vinyl they are all one voice, laying sound against sound, faces pale. Sing with one voice. The bed overfilling with them, so many shaved legs and perfumed necks piling in. The more he knows their details, their family sagas, the specific curves of their hip bones, their separate moans, the more they are one voice. Sabbath Queen we greet you as one. He is the Sabbath Queen all in white, flesh glowing against the gray sheets. The Shehina is the female aspect of our god-term, the queen of the sabbath who is the sabbath, the rest, the pause in God's week. Tanya only comes one Friday to make up a

Wednesday lesson she'd canceled for ballet recital and he is brisk. They are doing Hebrew grammar and like piano she never practices, somehow thinks she can fake through it and he never yells but ends halfway through the hour. "I've got a new really cool arrangement for L'chah Dodee we're gonna record tonight. Can I show you?"

Rubbing tongues and cunts, not fucking, doesn't want fucking. Can't think of fucking them without imagining the little rips and slender tears. They'd bleed home riding high on their new night licenses. The slow rubbery wetness of it hardening him, watching their lips ready for the scream of christ fucking christ yes, sliding across not in them. Josh on top of some girl, Josh short and swimming in her, Mike walking in on them and Josh's eyes joking back to him, promising to save something for him. Like just because the song is about drugs, the Eagles being totally about drugs, doesn't make it not about pain at the same time, you know. "Some dance to remember, some dance to forget." They harmonize, their breath unfresh, their voices gliding through him.

EVERYONE MOVES IN 1980

Tanya didn't realize it at the time, wrapped around her own family's shifting fortunes and a sudden urge to smush her toes in pink satin pointe shoes fourteen hours a day as she was, but after she left the Ithaca Association of Jewish Studies was absorbed by the conservative Temple Beth El with Rabbi Glass and his fully catered Judaism by numbers. Mike left, Renee left . . . she loses track of the rest, of where they left to. At the time she thinks Ithaca will leave her clean, wash off over the years as she rubs in other odors, larger cities. Seventeen, queen of the professionally alienated girls in black, insistently excitedly bored oh fucking bored by it all and the phone rings in the dorm room. "It's your mother. Did Michael Silverstein ever do anything to you?"

Wholesome and Natural

Scott O'Hara

Despite having had sex in a thousand public places over the years, I have never been arrested. Many of these encounters were illegal in other ways, as well: I was in a sodomy-law state, I was having sex with a seventeen-year-old, I didn't tell my partner that I had AIDS. (In Michigan, it doesn't even matter if you tell him: PWAs just aren't allowed to have sex. I took especial delight in flouting that particular barbarism.) Sex, I kept telling my partners—usually in nonverbal terms—is nothing to be ashamed of. Sucking dick through glory-holes is not immoral, antisocial, or aberrant. What's sick is the amount of energy our society pours into trying to repress those wholesome and natural desires.

I suppose I'm preaching to the perverted, here. None of my read-ers is liable to be surprised by any of these declarations. But I am continually amazed by how many gay men retain those lingering remnants of guilt and self-hatred: men who suspect they're "sex addicts" because they love to feel the sunlight on their backs while they're fucking someone, or because they go to dark and dirty movie theaters to watch guys jack off on stage. My entire life, looking back on it, has been devoted to telling these guys: NO! You are normal —it's the society around you that's fucked up.

Some people will roll their eyes and say, "Yeah, sure," when they read that I was doing pornflicks to try to heal gay men's libidos. Well, there's no doubt that I was doing it for other reasons, too. I'm an exhibitionist: I like being watched. The notion that my image would be preserved forever on celluloid or videotape was an intense thrill to me. I also just liked the physical act of playing with many of my partners: not all of them, of course, but some of those guys were lots of fun. Nevertheless, I have to insist that the primary motivation for me being up there in lights was to make guys feel good about themselves. When I could look out there into the audience and see men jerking off, looking up admiringly at me, I had to grin at them. These were my people: these men who were learning to be un- ashamed of their sexuality. I didn't just see them in the audience at the Campus Theater; I saw them at Land's End, and the Midtowne Spa, and everywhere else I "performed," whether for money or for personal satisfaction. I saw them, by proxy, in the stacks of letters I got as editor of *STEAM*: men who wrote to thank me for the af- firmation I'd given them. And they make me proud. I'm not a big booster of what has come to be called The Gay Community, but these men who I see in all these places are my community. Some are still struggling to come out, some are far less inhibited than I'll ever be, but what we share is the knowledge that sex *is* wholesome and natural. It doesn't need to be hidden. It won't harm the children. It's not an assault. It's a declaration of membership in the human race.

Children are not born with a sense of shame about sex, regardless of what the hellfire-and-brimstone types would like us to believe. Chil- dren of both sexes play with their genitalia—their own and those of playmates—freely, with no sense that it might be unacceptable to society. They don't restrict such activities to the bathroom, or under covers; small children are just as likely to start rubbing their crotches at the dinner table or in a social gathering. And Mother, shocked at this display of naturalness, will slap the little children's hands and send them to bed without supper. Eventually, of course, the kids get the message: touching themselves "down there" is wrong, pleasure is wrong, anything to do with penis, vagina, or asshole is dirty.

I don't even remember these lessons from my mother; they took place, I assume, before the dawn of recorded history. Being the fourth son in my family, I doubt that she was actually shocked by my behav- ior, but I'm sure she took draconian measures to stop it. Rather effec- tively, I guess: I do not recall playing with myself until I was ten, though my curiosity about other boys' peepees began much earlier.

All these things are about as natural as you can get. I sincerely hope that in the past thirty years, there has been some change in parental attitudes toward masturbation: parents who are capable of remembering the shame and guilt visited upon them by their own parents, and who don't want to repeat the cycle. I can remember, as early as age twelve, fantasizing about how I would raise my children, to free them from the ridiculous inhibitions I'd inherited. Casual household nudity figured prominently in this fantasy; and a common sleeping area, where parents (and I didn't limit myself to two, but frequently envisioned a communal household with multiple parents: I have to give credit for this idea to Robert A. Heinlein) and children would sleep in a massive puppy-pile. This thought gave me a warm and secure feeling. Today, if put into practice, it would give me fifty-to-life.

And that's the problem, obviously. Parental attitudes may be changing, slowly, but the legal system appears to be moving in the other direction. Sexuality of all sorts, especially juvenile sexuality, is becoming more and more off-limits. The definition of what constitutes sexual harassment has gone off the deep end. I'm sure most of the people who heard about that seven-year-old who gave his classmate a kiss on the cheek thought, "Oh, how sweet." A century ago, fifty years ago, even ten years ago, I think that would have been the reaction. Now, thanks to this new version of politically correct puritanism, any expression of affection is considered taboo, because it might lead to sex. We would be a healthier society if we could get over this phobia of touching, of affection—of sex.

I suppose I should be grateful to my parents. You see, they didn't tell me that hugging or kissing was bad; they just made it clear, by their own behavior, that it Wasn't Done. I never saw any affection between them; I don't believe either of them ever touched me, except in the most utilitarian way. Holding my hand when we crossed the street, that sort of thing. So on that incredible afternoon—April 16, 1977—when a man said to this trembling, shaking adolescent, "Let me hold you," the world burst into fireworks and flowers, and I didn't have the slightest doubt that what we were doing was right and wonderful. I did not have any sense of it being "immoral" or "unnatural"; it was the most natural thing in the world, the thing I'd been waiting for all my life. I cried. I cried for the years that I'd wasted in isolation, and the more years that I knew would pass before I could really join the human race. And possibly, just a little, I cried for my parents, who I somehow knew had never experienced anything like this. How could they? The only person they'd publicly admit to loving was Jesus.

Years went by. I knew, of course, that sex was not "supposed" to be a public act; but I don't recall ever having any doubts about its essential rightness. I knew, with a confidence that came from somewhere Other, that my parents were Wrong: deeply, intrinsically wrong. Not evil, but misled. Sex was good; sharing my body with another person was an affirmation of everything positive in life; and making a public display of that sexuality was one of the most basic ways in which I could improve the world. So I had sex in all the places where we're not supposed to do it: parks, beaches, bathhouses, bars, back alleys. Did I feel fear? You bet. It was clear to me, at even the tenderest age, that there were evil men in uniform out there who were devoted to the suppression of sex; and the thought of being in the grip of that gestapo was one of the most frightening things I could imagine. These are the ones I call the Antilife Patrol, the ones who, instead of intimacy and affection, merely crave control over other people. They are, and always have been, the enemy. They've arrested the producers of the films I've been in; they've arrested a friend of mine who had a mutually rewarding relationship with a child (with the approval of the child's parents); they would like to prevent magazines such as *STEAM* from being published. They have good reason to be afraid of sex: once people discover the potential for pleasure in their bodies, I think they become a lot less willing to submit to external authority.

It's my unwillingness to accept that authority at face value that has made me an effective "pleasure activist" (thank you, Annie Sprinkle)—and, at times, a lightning rod for criticism. I've come out in favor of sex on film, public sex, anonymous sex, intergenerational sex, Positive sex, and "unsafe" sex; in each case, I've raised someone's hackles. The bottom line is that I believe that sex is inherently good. The nice thing about the gay community, insofar as it exists, is that there has been some effort to accept sex as an integral part of life. The gay men I know are not ashamed of their sex lives: when they go out to a sexclub, I'll probably get a call the next day, with a vivid report of what went on. This casual attitude toward sex—this unwillingness to lie about, hide, or disguise our sexual cravings—is one of the primary "bonds" of my community.

My only regret is that this group of men is still not being given the chance to pass on these values to the next generation. I know they could do a helluva lot better job than my parents did.

Bad Plumbing

Katinka Hooijer

I'm twenty-eight years old and never remember having completely pain-free sex. Wait, I take that back—possibly in my first year of sexual activity, when the pain was the way to rate (or a minor consequence of) a good fuck. The sheer excitement of stiffboard banging, that sent him to cum heaven and me to burning vulva hell, seemed to be an OK trade-off for the power trip I got out of making someone shake and moan.

I finally couldn't deal with the pain. All I could think of was, what am I doing wrong? What is he doing wrong? Why does this thing, sex—the most beautiful, natural, healthy thing—send me into pain and frustration? Will the cycle of pain, denial, shame, anger make me a pervert, a nun, a lesbian, a prude? Where is it coming from? Why do I have it? Me: Miss Monogamy, Miss Safe Sex, Miss Annual Check-Up, Miss Don't Put Anything in Your Snatch Except a Dick or a Tampon, Miss I Wish I Could Fuck Without Emotional Attachment Like a Real Feminist.

Time to go to the doctor and demand an answer. Something besides "possibly you're having too rigorous sex," "try more lubrication," "try more foreplay," or "possibly you have a strain of bacterial vaginosis," from the uninformed but friendly people at Planned Parenthood. So I tried the University Health Clinic.

> Diagnosis: vulvodynia, i.e., chronic vulval discomfort characterized by burning, stinging, rawness, for which there is no obvious cause. Possible seminal fluid allergy, latex allergy, or contact dermatitis. Allergy testing suggested, negative Pap smear, negative bacterial cultures. An "offered" prohibition of sexual activity for a few weeks to break pain cycle until next visit.

Wear condoms, don't wear condoms, change detergent, throw away polyester underwear, go off the Pill. After about six weeks of allergy testing myself, I was still burning. I abstained for three weeks and then tried riding my boyfriend. Fuck me. This isn't working. I followed all the rules: lots of lube, soft gentle entry, minimal friction. Fuck me, this really hurts. My doctor was just as frustrated as I, but not nearly as horny. She got me in with a part-time gynecologist. My Pap was negative (again) and I should be happy. But somehow my clean record made all of this more confusing and scary.

I developed deeper pelvic pain. Maybe it was just stress. The gyno thought I might have endometriosis and surgery was the only way to diagnose. How convenient, he makes an extra five grand with this disease and I might not even have it. The pussy pain may or may not be related to the endometriosis. I was so desperate I went ahead with the surgery. The physical pain was nothing compared to the mindfuck all the non-fucking gave me. Antidepressants were prescribed, but I didn't need those—I wasn't some pathetic sniveling Beverly Hills chick who couldn't lose that extra five pounds.

> Preoperative diagnosis: vulvar vestibulitis and severe pelvic pain.
>
> Postoperative diagnosis: endometriosis.
>
> The patient was brought to the operating room and placed in the supine position and given adequate general anesthesia . . . attention was then turned toward the abdomen where using number 11 blade a radial incision was placed inside her umbilicus. A 10 mm trocar and sheath were inserted into her abdominal cavity . . . she was inflated with 2-3 liters of carbon dioxide gas. The right uterosacral ligament appeared to be free of lesions and adhesions. The posterior cul-de-sac appeared to be free of adhesions. However, on the left side toward the left uterosacral ligament there appeared to be small endometrial implants measuring approximately 6 to 10 in number, approximately 1-2 mm in diameter . . . while using an endo coagulator at 120 degrees Celsius setting, her endometrial implants were cauterized in their entirety.

That operation was so fucking weird. I was in and out of the hospital in six hours. I felt pretty good for a while but that night I felt like someone had hit me in the stomach with a baseball bat. A week later I was black and blue and my stitches itched like hell. I'd been putting the topical hydrocortisone on for two weeks for the vulvar pain. My poor lips. The cream seemed to help at first, but then it burned more than ever. "It's supposed to burn at first." This was wrong. I just stopped this shit altogether. Since I was going on vacation for a while, I was excited to see if the surgery had worked. Be positive. Mind over body.

I had a flare-up of some sort. It'd been about five months since the surgery and I guess the pelvic pain was better. My snatch felt like someone had shoved a weed-whacker up it. I was on antibiotics for the third time for some vaginal bacteria. I got a yeast infection from the antibiotics fucking with my immune system, then I got another flare-up from the vaginal suppositories for the yeast. All in all, life sucked. I dropped out of school for the semester because I couldn't sit on my box for more than twenty minutes without itching and burning. I couldn't wear jeans anymore. I decided to allow myself to be depressed and spend the rest of my life in the bathtub.

My gyno became a state senator. Good. He was too squeamish to be doing pelvic exams. "Oh, I'll be quick, I hate these as much as you do." Thanks a lot, Doc, for being so thorough. Apparently he was so busy campaigning that he didn't do his homework on vaginal pain syndromes:

> Vulvar vestibulitis or vulvar pain syndrome remains an enigma because so many questions about the disorder are left unanswered. The patient is often misdiagnosed and treated with therapies such as topical steroids, which exacerbate the condition. This experience aggravates gynecologist and patient alike and frequently damages the patient/physician relationship.[1]

No shit. Especially when the physician damages the patient. Asshole.

I finally got in with a specialist of vulvar diseases through an urgent referral from my general practitioner, after a three-month wait. I went to a homeopathic physician in the meantime. According to ayurvedic medicine, I had too much fire. Which reminded me of Zorba the Greek, who bragged, "I have enough fire in me to devour the world, so I fight." I love that guy. So I fought. Fought the urge to eat hot foods. Fought the urge to pity myself, and fought the urge to blame every damn thing for my illness. I probably had too much fire because I was angry as fuck. I had to cut out the spicy foods in my diet, which meant I had to stop getting wasted, since the Mexican butt-flush brunch/hangover cure was no longer allowable.

I started feeling better. I canceled my appointment with the specialist. I felt shitty again. Rescheduled with the specialist. I was on fucking fire. I felt like I'd just sat on a hibachi. I was waging war on my body. I was pissed so I didn't take my remedies, I ate Mexican food, and I drank heavily. Then I pitied my body. I pampered it. I took every herbal bath, tried every remedy, drank every tea, and swallowed every tincture to bring some comfort.

I cried a lot. I tried to respect myself and my snatch. It was getting more and more difficult for my boyfriend to deal with my moods. It was getting more and more difficult for me to deal with my moods. I tried an acupuncturist. She consoled me by saying that in China many women have this problem and, with the right herbs, the liver and spleen can be balanced. There was hope.

The acupuncture was quite relaxing. Once in a while she'd hit a point that sent a shock throughout my whole body. When she hooked me up to the electricity I felt as though I was floating; I felt really calm. I took a foul-tasting herbal combination she special ordered for me. Making a tea from it was definitely out of the question; it made me puke. I mixed it with honey and swallowed it.

The acupuncture and herbs were not really helping. I believe that if the doctor had caught the problem before I got more fucked up from the steroid ointments and antibiotics, she might have been able to help. I guessed that since Western medicine had been part of the cause, it would have to be part of the cure.

March 1995. Finally someone who knew what she was doing. This doc interviewed me for over an hour. Then had my boyfriend come in and asked him some questions about his sexual history. Questions I had already answered for her because I *knew* he would never *lie* to me, especially anything which would affect the state of my health. Well, when she asked him—with all her degrees and her awards framed on the wall behind her—his answers were different. For some reason the questions were more legitimate and more urgent coming from her. He said his previous girlfriend had thought she had chlamydia, and he said he had been tested for it. He said at one point he'd had warts or lesions or something, but the tests had never been positive. What an asshole. Why couldn't he have been honest with me? I knew the complexity and vagueness of all these tests. I was living it. None of those tests are completely accurate. Why didn't he feel that he could've trusted me? I wouldn't have judged him. Shit, I didn't think I needed to get his medical history on paper. I made him go in that week for a full checkup. He turned out clean. Lucky for him.

Whatever I had was not related to STDs and was not cancerous. My "disorder" was very severe and the doc could only attempt the physical exam in awe. "I can't believe this. I don't even want to touch you. There's no way I can even insert a speculum. How can you sit down?"

"I squirm a lot."

"How can you urinate?"

"It usually burns and I have to pour cold water on my crotch."

"You are very brave. We'll get you through this, angel."

I liked that she called me angel. She gave me Kleenexes when I cried. She acknowledged my pain and didn't judge me. She promised to help me. Her nurse held my hand. But I got charged.

My Student Association president, vice president, and women's issues director, plus my Student Health Center doctor all wrote letters to my insurance company. Unfortunately, my insurance company was a gigantic asshole. Maybe my condition was unusual and unreasonable, but after I'd been paying them to cover 80 percent of my medical bills, they ended up willing to barely cover 40 percent.

For the next month, I soaked in medicated baths daily, applied compresses twice daily, missed work, and worried about how to pay for the bills. I also applied estrogen cream to help the vaginal tissues heal.

One month later, my second visit. I was a little more comfortable but still couldn't endure an exam. I broke down and began taking the antidepressants. I knew it was getting increasingly difficult to deal with the burning vulva bitch from hell so that's part of why I took antidepressants. It was a small dosage and supposed to just be for the nerve pain, supposedly it wouldn't affect my personality. Too bad, I could've used a personality makeover.

Third visit. I went off the antidepressants because I couldn't sleep or shit properly (two things I still get some pleasure out of). After five months of compresses, Estrace cream, and medicinal baths I was finally to the point where my doctor could get in to take some biopsies. I never realized an anesthetic could hurt so much: imagine getting a needle in your inner labia or a shot in your dickhole. I couldn't feel the actual cutting of the skin, but I could feel the tugging of skin when she sewed up the two cuts she made on the upper half of my vulva. My pain tolerance is quite high, but just the thought of having my pussy cut freaked me out. Talk about an invasion of privacy. But even with this, the most personal of illnesses, I wanted to tell everyone. I wanted everyone to know the pain I was enduring. A pain you couldn't see. A pain associated with morals. Pussy pain = lots of sex = lots of partners = high risk = STDs = pelvic inflammatory disease = she deserves it, that whore.

> Pathology Consultation Report: diagnosis; tissue, "subclitoral/ vestibular area," biopsy: superficial acute and chronic inflammation with erosion and inflammatory cell exocytosis.

Geniuses. Did they really have to cut my vulva to figure that out? I mean they could have just asked me. The biopsy did confirm a lichenoid disorder which may be related to getting canker sores in my mouth. I have "ulcers" on my vulva that flare up and the cells of the vaginal tissues are constantly shedding (that sounds better than eroding). Actually, it all sounds disgusting.

My boyfriend and I spent two months in Europe to "get away." We made love the first night of our trip and then he ignored my body for the next two months. I had a flare-up the whole time. I dumped him the night we got back.

> Although a pathophysiologic association between diseases of the skin and emotion have always been suggested, it was not until 1989 when a physiologic mechanism was identified. Stress often accompanies psychologic disorders such as severe marital conflicts, somatization disorders, chronic pain syndromes, and depressive syndromes.[2]

It's weird how straight people define sex. Sex is penis into vagina and involves male ejaculation. Him getting off and spraying her walls. This is how I thought of sex. I felt cheated because I hadn't had dick for so long. I felt like I was cheating my partner because he missed out on my warm, wet walls. Sure, oral sex. But that really didn't count as sex, did it?

A new lover. He liked my body and appreciated it. He knew how to kiss, how to touch. But I wouldn't trust him with my snatch. Only I was allowed down there. His body felt nice and warm and he made me feel sexy again, despite my broken sex organ. He was comfortable enough with himself that he could whack off in front of me and pay me enough attention to make it all worthwhile.

I couldn't stand it. I really needed more of an emotional bond with a lover. Obviously a good fuck was no longer the main objective. My emotions were, however, in a state of instability. With the advice of my doctor, boyfriends were no longer an option. I was better off alone. That way I didn't have to deal with feelings of inadequacy and sexual frustration. Plus I had the bathtub and my loyal shower hose to make me feel like a woman. Hopefully I wouldn't go blind.

It'd been a long year since my biopsy. I accidentally got a boyfriend, against doctor's orders. I tried to keep him off for months, but he was too persistent. I told him about my disease. He was suspicious. He thought it was a good line to avoid sex on the first date. But I really think he thought I had AIDS. He did ask me a few times.

I "failed all conservative therapy" and was going to have a vulvar vestibulectomy. In real words, having the lower half of my pussy removed. I had mixed feelings about this. I wanted to try more, less invasive, alternative therapies, but also didn't want my condition to worsen. Basically, I was just tired and desperate. The surgery might or might not help. There was a 40 percent chance I'd still feel like shit and sex was not guaranteed—not to mention childbirth. Also I would still have the lichen planus (vulvar skin disorder). My doctor was quite optimistic that the removal of the vestibular glands (in the lower part of the vulva) would alleviate much of my pain, since it was these glands that became inflamed by the lichenoid disorder. No glands, no inflammation? Hopefully.

Preoperative diagnosis: vulvar vestibulitis and lichen planus vaginitis.

Operative procedure: vulvar vestibulectomy. The areas of pain were identified. The patient was positioned in the dorsolithotomy position, sterilely prepared and draped. With a marking pen, the vestibular was outlined from the lateral urethra on one side to the lateral urethra on the other side, and the area from the hymen to Hart's line was colored with a pen. The circumscribing incision was made, and the superficial vestibule was resected. The vagina was undermined posteriorly, and the flap was pulled out to make sure it fit correctly to the vagina. A posterior vaginal bridge was transected. The vestibule was then reconstructed using absorbable stitches of 4-0 material. Cautery and sutures were used for hemostasis, and good hemostasis was obtained. The undermined vaginal epithelium was pulled out posteriorly to make a smooth and cosmetically acceptable introitus. There were no complications, and the patient was sent in good condition to the post anesthesia recovery area.

After the surgery I had to take a pee before I was allowed to leave. A nurse helped me up and took me down the hall to the toilet. I was numb down to my knees where I suddenly felt something warm and wet. A steady stream of blood dyed my socks bright red. For some reason, I didn't respond to this at all. In the bathroom the nurse cleaned me up and apologized for not getting a wheelchair. My best friend was waiting for me when I got back. I wanted to stop for ice cream, but passed out for the half-hour drive home. Anesthesia rocks.

For three days I could barely walk. I couldn't look at my wound. My boyfriend kept an eye on my pussy for me. He was the one who helped me heal. He didn't mind that there was never any penetration or banging. Somehow he sensed, somehow he knew, that we would not have intercourse in the months to come even after my expected recovery date. But he still had a way of making me feel desirable just by looking at me the right way. Isn't it strange that I have felt the sexiest with a man who had never experienced the wrath of my sexual apparatus?

One month after surgery I was healing okay. The rest of my stitches were pulled out. She did miss a few because when I was at Six Flags Great America some of them worked their way out. That's always a surprise, finding stitches in your underpants. My hymen was completely gone now. And it looked like my right lip was shorter than the rest. I guess that's what they called a "cosmetically acceptable introitus." It wasn't bad enough for me to make mad cash in the porn/freak industry and not good enough to ride my man. What a rip-off.

Another month went by and I was in horrible shape. My doctor couldn't believe how bad I looked—it was worse than before my surgery. I went to Walgreen's Pharmacy with a new prescription since all my refills from my old one were used up. The charge was fifty-six bucks. I knew that couldn't be right because all year I'd been paying less than half that for the same prescription. Oops, the pharmacist made a mistake ten months ago and gave me Anusol suppositories—not Anusol HC (a steroid). So I'd been on the wrong fucking medication for almost a year. I was supposed to have been on steroid therapy but I really wasn't. Hmmm. Could this have caused a little confusion on the part of my doctor? Is this why I didn't respond to "conventional therapy"? Because I wasn't even on it?!

Think positive, at least you caught the mistake. Think positive, you can help so many women through your testimony. And then again, think positive, your doctors gained knowledge through your pain. Fuck everyone. All I wanted was to make love to my man.

Tears of self-pity, frustration, and anger went into even the final draft of this story, and it is a story I'm still living. Currently, I am still in pain. I'm far away from my lover, but I hope one day to fuck the living shit out of him. I deserve it. The only thing that makes publicizing my disease worthwhile (besides in a medical report, case study, or research paper) is that women with these problems will realize that these feelings are not in their heads, they are real.

Please don't be a passive patient, demand answers. Don't trust everything your doctor says, demand proof. Please don't wear panty liners or pads with "patented" layers of synthetic fibers that "remove moisture to keep you dry." (Go ahead and sue me.) Please don't use feminine hygiene products with deodorants or feminine deodorant sprays for that "fresh feeling." (Go ahead and sue me.) You'll just fuck up your natural chemical balance, you clog up your vestibular glands with synthetic chemicals. And you'll fuck up your sex life, so take care of your plumbing.

NOTES

1. J. Paavonen. "Diagnosis and Treatment of Vulvodynia," *Annals of Medicine,* 27(2), April 1995, 175-181.

2. Michael S. Baggish and John R. Mikes, "Vulvar Pain Syndrome: A Review," *CME Review,* Article 23, 50(8), 1995, 423-433.

Girlfriends, Boyfriends, Dykes, or Fags?

Jaron Kanegson

Recently I prowled around on stage under blue lights, picked up a cute gay boy, and got my dick sucked. This may have surprised some of my friends, since they know me as a dyke. So what was I doing on stage, pretending to be a fag cruising in a park?

Before trying to answer that question, I should clarify a few points. My dick was the twelve-dollar Duke model, a black rubber dildo, strapped on underneath a pair of briefs with a black leather harness. My girlfriend, Gretchen, who like me looks as much like a young gay boy as a dyke, was the person sucking my dick. And the context was a performance piece at LunaSea, a women's performance space in San Francisco.

So why did I do it? What possessed me to get on stage in front of friends and strangers and drop my drawers? Reason number one was probably just that I thought it would be fun. Gretchen and I had previously enjoyed some similar cocksucking scenes, both at home and at public sex parties. Since we both have an exhibitionist streak, having a captive audience was right up our alley.

But, there was more to it than that. The scene began with me cruising Gretchen as she sat on a park bench with Madonna playing in the background, and culminated with Gretchen on her knees delivering a quick blow job. As such, it was an appropriate prelude to a piece Gretchen read about gender identity. Our performance gave us both a chance to demonstrate aspects of ourselves that can be difficult to explain in words.

Gretchen and I look enough like fags that getting hit on in the Castro is a frequent experience for both us, and each of us has at times been the crush object of otherwise staunchly gay men. One fag friend of mine even told me that watching us perform our cocksucking scene led him to develop an attraction to Gretchen. I was only slightly surprised, since her all-American blondish blue-eyed boy look tends to get her butt pinched in men's bars. As for me, I more frequently experience cruisey stares that turn sheepish when I smile back, since smiling somehow lends a more feminine cast to my features. One prolonged gazer, however, simply confessed to being a "chicken hawk" when I pointedly mentioned I was female, kept right on staring, and went on to point me out to his friends!

The bottom line is that I don't merely get hit on by gay men—a significant portion of my gender identity is built around the idea that, on some level, I *am* one. Performing on stage looking and acting like a gay man allowed me to convey an aspect of my gender that the words "woman," "dyke," and even "butch" really don't convey. Although I felt vulnerable and exposed, I knew that I was acting out a part of myself, not a parody of someone else. Part of me is a fag, and that was the part I let show that night.

One reason I relished getting to show my male/fag self on stage is that I often receive negative feedback about my appearance from people who find my gender presentation too masculine. In women's rest rooms, especially outside of San Francisco, I am frequently laughed at or asked to leave. Sometimes people, even other queer women, assume that I cut my hair short and wear masculine clothing to "prove" how much of a dyke I am. My mother has even offered me money to grow out my hair.

Not only do people sometimes wrongly assume that I dress as I do to put my sexual orientation "in their face," but random strangers seem to feel compelled to comment on my appearance. The last time I was in Boston, an older white woman in a rest room angrily demanded to know why I wanted to fool people. As soon as I returned to the Bay Area, an Asian woman in a business suit called me a "faggot" on the street in Berkeley.

While Gretchen has had many similar experiences on her own, it sometimes seems that we attract even more negative attention when we are together, perhaps because we resemble young fags. Recently, for example, we made the mistake of venturing into the women's room at Nieman Marcus in Palo Alto, because we weren't in the mood to deal with waiting in line for the stall in the men's room (where neither of us ever gets so much as a funny look). We were treated with such hostility that one woman felt compelled to apologize to us for "people's idiocy" as we left. In a separate incident in a parking lot in Castroville, we narrowly escaped a car full of guys who seemed intent on beating us up.

Incidents such as these are obviously extremely disturbing, and the apparently easy solution might be to simply change my appearance. What seems to escape many people, however, is not only that I have a right to dress as I wish, but that I choose to dress in a way that makes me feel comfortable and attractive.

Ironically, I can't be considered butch in the traditional sense of the word. I'm masculine in an effeminate way—a pansy butch. For a long time, I found this oxymoron difficult to understand. For years, I tried to figure out how straight strangers took me for a man, while many dykes thought I was "femme."

Part of my confusion came from the fact that I've always been attracted to masculine women. Like a still-clueless gay man who can't understand how he can both feel attracted to men and still be one, I didn't comprehend how I could be so incontrovertibly attracted to butch women, and still be butch myself. For a while I simply maintained both that I was not a femme, and that I must have been a gay man in my last life, even if I didn't know what I was in this one.

Finally, a friend introduced me to the term "boy-dyke," which is used to describe a female-born dyke who looks like and/or identifies in part as a boy or man. I decided that I was a boy-dyke fag, a boy-dyke attracted to other butch women, and have been able to make more sense of the whole thing ever since.

I now know many other people who, while labeled as "female" at birth, identify as butches, boy-dykes, FTMs (female-to-male transsexuals) or somewhere in between. I've also realized that while I may not be transsexual, or even traditionally butch, I do fall somewhere on a broad spectrum of gender expression that society labels transgender.

Someone who doesn't worry about gender identity might wonder what exactly is so important about figuring all this out. But our culture clearly punishes those who don't follow gender rules. The unprosecuted rape and subsequent murder of twenty-one-year-old Brandon Teena (also known as Teena Brandon) on December 31,

1993 in Falls City, Nebraska, which occurred after his status as a female-bodied person living as a man was exposed, is just one example.

Despite the hatred and potential violence gender benders experience in our culture, it is still difficult to find the words to describe ourselves. Our vocabulary is limited in terms of the words we have to describe gender, which makes gender variations nameless and invisible. In contrast, in her book *Transgender Warriors*, Leslie Feinberg quotes the Navajo scholar Wesley Thomas, who has categorized at least forty-nine different gender identities in traditional Navajo culture.[1]

For myself, the word "woman" has never adequately described my gender, and while the word "dyke" brought me a little closer, it was still not enough. Finding and developing further vocabulary has helped me to better understand myself. It has also helped me realize that I have the right to my own gender identity. I should be able to wear the clothes that I want to wear, cut my hair short, or even modify my body with hormones or surgery if I wanted to make that choice.

While I do have a partially male identity, I also have a strong identity as a person who has lived in the box of "woman." I am a committed feminist, and I consider gender-bending a feminist and freeing act. However, I can see how someone might misunderstand me labeling part of myself as "male-identified" antifeminist or even woman-hating.

"Male-identified" is one of the worst possible feminist slurs. I myself have used it to describe women I feel put the needs of men as a group before the needs of women as a group. But I don't believe that having a nontraditional gender identity makes me, or anyone else, antiwoman.

Everyone has both masculine and feminine traits, regardless of the sex we are assigned to at birth. I have many friends born into "women's" bodies, who embrace feminism and female liberation, yet who identify partially or primarily as male. Thinking of myself as partly male does not mean that I do not value the qualities our society has labeled "female," of the people our society calls "women." Nor does it necessarily mean that I even like most men.

As a group, traditional straight men tend to make me nervous—I don't trust them to treat me with respect.

Until our society has a better understanding of gender, and a much broader vocabulary to describe gender identity, it will remain all too easy to assign people to limiting and unequal categories. That is why I relished getting on stage and demonstrating that Gretchen and I, while dykes, are also fags, and girlfriends who are simultaneously boyfriends. Of course, getting to have my dick sucked in front of all those people didn't hurt either.

NOTE

1. Feinberg, Leslie. *Transgender Warriors: Making History from Joan of Arc to RuPaul.* Boston: Beacon Press, 1996, p. 27.

Scenes from a Culture of Masochism

T. A. King

In the basement of Chicago's Hellfire clubhouse we negotiate the terms through which our leather gear will become something other than cowskin, denim, and metal. Our flesh, too, is waiting to become other than its mundane meanings. Here we drink beer, laugh, exchange gossip, and trade techniques. Here it matters who we are, how we witness each other, where we need to be later. But heading up the stairs into the playspace we will adjust our flesh and drop our words. The scripts we have negotiated will operate through our bodies. As we cross the threshold, we turn our cowskin and metal over to something other, something belonging to the space itself. We submit our flesh as surfaces on which the space will inscribe traditions, technologies, disciplines.

This is not to say we are passively written. We have already written the space; hundreds of men before us have already written the space. Our gestures, our movements, our encounters take their place within this writing that exists outside and beyond us and which we rewrite through our pleasures.

Upstairs a circle of men form an audience for the top's reenactment of his bottom's pleasure. The bottom has been hooded and now lies quietly on a board suspended by ropes from the ceiling. The top binds him to the board with ropes in a crisscross pattern and then begins to attach clamps to the rings in his nipples, cock, and scrotum. We watch the bottom's belly move in and out with his deep and rhythmic breathing. The top ties a series of lines to the clamps and then strings the lines to anchors along the wall so that they pull on his bottom's flesh. We watch the bottom breathe. The top strings line through the D-rings in the hood and binds the bottom's head to the board. He lights candles one by one and drips them along his bottom's flesh, defining its surface. The bottom's breathing moves under the new skin his master has made for him. The top lets a pool of hot wax form on his bottom's belly and fixes a candle there, letting it burn down in his boy's navel. The bottom takes on a new ego, a new bodily envelope to project for the group of men watching him. The top tightens the lines and as the candle burns low, jerks his boy's dick deftly and familiarly. Almost unnecessarily: the scene is an act of care re-creating them both. A very slight spasm and the bottom becomes his top's bottom again. We wait for the hood to come off and for the look of difference the bottom will wear with his face. We wait there so that the bottom can see his submission in the eyes of the group.

He says, My prostate requires an audience. I show it to you, for I am insufficient to my pleasure. It takes at least three men to make a bottom—or a top.

In the basement of the Hellfire clubhouse we might ask you: Will you let yourself become a spectacle? Or is pleasure a sign of your privacy and self-possession, that which above all else should not require a witness? We will denigrate your separate personhood and relocate your body and its pleasures in a space already occupied by other men. Here in this playspace we exercise a structure of training, technique, and reiteration that does not belong to the self nor expresses it. We cannot fully assimilate or map the event or possess its space. We each have our acquired techniques and our positions in the space; but our pleasure requires a collective scene in which these techniques may be put into play. My pleasure is outside myself in the collective space. A bottom is a collective playspace. As is a top.

He says, The eyes of the leather bottom are black and bottomless and they take me inside. The longing his eyes show is not his; it belongs somewhere else. I do not know where I will go when the bottom takes me into his eyes I blindfold him I make him look down.

He says, I put on the boots, the chaps; I am playing out another man's desire. The cockring pushing out your balls; you are the image of another man's desire. The gauntlets and motorcycle cap; we are reenacting another man's desire, one neither of us can own (although we smell and taste like it). The fetish is not ours; we fit ourselves to it.

Toys: public sex, but reconstituted "at home," by myself or with you or others. Playing with our toys we make ourselves visible, but within a field of vision to which we cannot be equivalent. Who is (watching us) having sex? "Do we need to be top or bottom when it's just us?" Is the jockstrap I make you put on "just" a fetish? I will make you see yourself as you are seen by another man (not-me). The dildo is a field of possibility among hands and holes. We do not make each other whole but make each other the scene on which the practices particular to this place are enacted. You are uncomfortable with this; you feel that sex should be the expression of your fullest being; you love it when I hold your head down in my lap. The spectacle we occupy is the fleshly part of desire.

The baths, the bushes, the dunes, the tearooms, the sexclubs: we know that a man belongs here if he can be seen as here to be had. He has to know and give the signal: potential penetrability. Through the eyes, through the nose, through his fingers: in the view of other men he will project his body as a surface receptive to my look. Cruising: you know what it means when a man lets his gaze lock with yours—Take me in. He will have learned where and how to play through dog-eared cruising guides, telephone hotlines, invitations passed out in the streets or bars, advertisements, and calendar listings in gay newspapers and Web pages. He will have learned the signals from an experienced friend or by reading *The Joy of Gay Sex*, already passed from hand to mouth. He will be ready to assume the position of an apprentice to the space. In the playspace our history is an asset, the accumulation of techniques and scenarios. Perhaps the animus against public sex rests on the anxious and rather accurate description of public sex as a kind of pederasty—an experienced man passing on his knowledge and his techniques to an inexperienced one, a novice, an initiate.

In the basement of the Hellfire clubhouse the bottom stands attentively behind the top. The top is seated across from us and he is at ease. We drink beer and chat; we only chat with the top. We address the bottom indirectly through his top, sustaining the couple's mutual construction of the field of vision and publicizing our competence. Thereby we make the top; we make the bottom. In the normative public sphere this couple might go unremarked. Their performance might disappear or rather pass as another performance (that of invisibility). The presence of a willing and knowing audience makes their relationship visible to the group and to themselves.

In the dunes lining Herring Cove Beach in Provincetown, nudity and public sex are illegal, but a well-rehearsed relay of male voices warns of approaching rangers. We suit up; they drive by; we strip down again. In the summer of 1994, some fabulous unmarked men had even built an entire watch station in the dunes—a faerie palace constructed of flotsam, jetsam, stones, and salvaged wood and topped by a flagpole. A counter-ranger station, alternative public sphere. When the flag was out, all was safe. But who was watching (for) us? Who cut those trails for us in the woods, clearing the underbrush where we cruise, making a space around the oak where we meet to jerk off in groups? In spring 1996 a friend sent me an e-mail advisory that the cruising area in the Stoneham Fells in Massachusetts would probably come to the attention of the police, now that so many married men were going there for quick blow jobs. Those men were recognized as "straight" by their ignorance of the etiquette proper to the space. They thought they could use the space without being changed by it. They thought they would not be seen by the space.

This is not to say that deep down they were "really gay." Signals, roles, and performance techniques do not follow naturally from or mandate an identity. The fetish and the space take precedence over identity categories. These are not private spaces for and about gay men. Public sex spaces maneuver the players who pass through them into something other than their other public identities. You will not belong to the space if you do not let yourself become different from yourself there. Around the fetish a metonymy of bodies occurs, and this syncopation of bodies in space does not require or reproduce a single, continuous self.

He says, Is this the real me, or is he tickling my fancy? So what if I am ventriloquizing experiences which do not belong to me. Even my presentness in this performance, on this page, cannot be said to belong to me. For it is your pleasure in reading that has constituted my presence.

We have learned to say: Sex is an altruistic and purposeful relation with the other. Pleasures establish a relationship between two and are a means for mutually authenticating each other.[1] I want to feel validated by your orgasm. I want to recognize my name in your moans. By mapping the pursuit of pleasure onto the public sphere, we tie "the public interest" to the relations between two knowable and separate selves. Sex is the public sphere—the domain of our mutual interests as private subjects—experienced as the pleasures of the body. Despite the intensity of our belief in the privacy of sexuality, sex has provided the experiential interface through which we make our membership in a public sphere known, felt in our bodies.[2]

All sex is public property; but "public sex" changes the emphasis from the witnessing of "private" desire to the witnessing of acts moving away from the private self toward a space, rhythm, and movement that is not self. In group sex, I multiply the scenes of pleasure rather than contribute to the affirmation of (my) selfhood and (your) otherness. Here, the other and the same become roles specific to the space. Public sex, group sex, sex with friends and strangers: these require no investment in or declaration of my *individual* self but only my commitment to the *collective* space. Sex outside relationships (among strangers and friends) constitutes only a temporary and local form of *social* organization. The continuity of any such organization (the continuity of pleasure) is ensured by the preservation of the collective space; but the space itself has an open and provisional form enabling improvisation and revision. Unlike the heterosexual family, which must reproduce itself at the level of individual desire, the continuity of public sex space does not require any likeness between my desire and the form of the space, between "who I am" and what I can *do*.

Disclosures and confessions provide the basic structure of a perverse encounter: Have you wanted? Yes, I have wanted, I have always wanted. But the perverse confession need not point inward to the truth of one's being. The perverse confession points instead to its own status as a performance calculated to produce future pleasures. Entering perverse space will not make a man of you. Entering the playspace enacts a discontinuity of the self, a giving over of privacy to the collective space. To confess, moreover, is not to acquiesce to the top. It is the space alone that draws the confession from you. The confession enters into and replays relations of power that exceed both top and bottom, voyeur and exhibitionist. The power that is pleasure is not the power of one over the other, for we never have that power in fetish play and are never convinced that we do. The very proliferation of manuals, guidebooks, rules, techniques, safe words, demonstrations, and discussion groups ensures that. Nor is it just a question of whether replaying already existing power relations reaffirms them. Rather the collective enunciation of the space calculates the difference of the self that enters into and reperforms the techniques it acquires there. Fetish play is the power to coproduce a space of pleasure discontinuous from the spaces of private sexualities.

The "dominant public sphere" maintains its hegemony by representing itself as exclusive, seamless, and homogeneous. Gay men's sexualization of space is not a production of safe space for gay men, nor is it the production of exclusively "gay space." Playspaces are not alternative spaces existing alongside dominant public space (as if, Cindy Patton reminds us, there are sufficient pieces of the spatial pie to go around[3]). Rather, they are (temporary or permanent) respatializations of existing public space, rearticulations of boundaries that occur when the official map of that space is revealed to be a fiction.[4] Playspaces queer the fiction that public spaces express the inevitability of private identity or require performances of hetero-, homo-, and bi-normativity. Playspaces demonstrate that sexual identities mutually constitute each other through the public disavowal of other possible uses of bodies.

To argue against a model of sexual relations as acts of altruism or pastoral care for "the other" is not to suggest, as Leo Bersani has done, that sexual activity is inherently "anticommunal, antiegalitarian, antinurturing, antiloving."[5] Group or public sex is not a practice of self-actualization but a means for establishing collective space. Collective sexual activity operates outside the psychologists' binaries of self and other. Misunderstanding this invariably casts gay male sexuality, which has visibly used sex as the means of collective identity formation, as immature, narcissistic, and inadequately other-directed. Reviews of porn videos in gay papers, the public sex experiences reported in *STEAM* or *First Hand,* and exhibitionism on the Net all construct eroticism as something that happens, not between two men, but collectively among a performance community. Often when we enter a cyberspace we are told the number of visitors who have already been there. The space has been well traversed; there are cum marks on the floor. When I visited on May 7, 1999, I noted that 156,563 others had already downloaded CyberCricket's body since the first of January; over three quarters of a million had checked him out in 1998 (http://members.home.net/scootchl.). Toaph's erotic portfolios online make him among the most famous exhibitionists in modern history. (http://www.actwin.com/topah/bronch.html). Toaph's exhibitionist pages not only produce queer cyberspace but explicitly queer other spaces than the fiber-optic cables mapping our world. Toaph's self-portraits are accompanied by erotic autobiographies locating his exhibitionism in a network of spaces and encounters *offline* and presenting his *online* activity as an opportunity for radically altering those spaces. His narratives show that even the most normalized public spheres have always provided space for perverse performances. By identifying those spaces and sharing techniques Toaph makes future encounters possible. Because it is geared toward the production of alternative public spheres, rather than the affirmation of self, Toaph's exhibitionism on the Net is a profoundly *communal* and *antinarcissistic* act. To care for "the other" is to care for the spaces of (his) pleasure.

The online exhibitionist does of course post an image of himself as he imagines others would like to see him; he hopes his visitors will confirm that they have been aroused. But the asynchronicity of homepage interactions or nonsimultaneous e-mail sex prevents any single encounter between a voyeur and an exhibitionist and substitutes a multiplicity of encounters occurring in unpredictable spaces at unforeseen times.[6] In asynchronous sex I have no control over how the supplement I produce to imagine myself and project my self-image will be used by others, for I am not there. Nor do I demand the other to care for *me*, but the *space* which proliferates beyond us both. Indeed, the technology of the computer itself remains radically other to my desire; and yet the inassimilable means, for instance, by which the image (my supplement, my face) downloads on another's screen can be in itself a pleasure (the pleasure of frustration and anticipation, the tease of the striptease). This is the thrill of a lack of mastery over, a failure of confirmation by the mutuality of gazes. Signing on or signing off is signing into a series of conjunctions over which I have no control. I cannot predict how thousands of men will occupy and use the space: one man is jerking off on my face; an other is making a thick description of my supplement for a research paper; another other is investigating the necessity of censoring the trace of our interactions. Just as we can never finally control the images we post, so we can never fully elicit the images we see. We can only stop downloading an image and move on to another. One cannot see the other in order to see one's self, because "the other" is not "there"; only the supplement occupies the same space and the present tense. There can be no fascist imposition of my ego on the space of asynchronicity.

The fetish is a practice of the space between my body and those of other men, present or absent. A supplement to both of us, a relation exceeding both of us, the fetish makes my body appear but always in the field of another man. The fetish makes his body appear to me and engages me in a performance which does not belong to me. The fetish draws eyes, hands, and cocks outside the ego space (that projected picture of ourselves we are always trying to lay on others) and into another space. The fetish is a performance that does not belong to either of us but is the evidence of our mutual relatedness to a space and to a set of techniques.

At J's Hangout in New York, he sits on a ledge off to one side, his pants around his ankles, immobilizing his legs and framing his public nakedness. His erection lies against his abdomen; a dozen stainless steel rings extend his ballsack virtuosically. The spectacle touches me; I touch back. This (re)formulation of flesh through metal, at once ungiving and yet mobile and musical like a dozen bracelets on a diva's wrist, commands my look. I accept and approve the supplement through which he makes himself visible to me. Through this practice of his body he appears as difference from his body. The supplement (re)writes embodiment as the collective practice of two or more men. His rendering of flesh into fetish—miming a technology that belongs elsewhere—he offers to the dozen or so clothed men cruising the bar. His is practiced flesh, a spectacle of discipline, endurance, and projection. It requires something of my look and commands my hand. I am the top for him; he is the bottom for me. This spectacle of duration places us together in the present of our performance.

This is the agency of the fetish: it is put out there to elicit a practice of the space among performers (more than two), or rather my entry into a space where an unnumbered number of men have already been. For these rings which look at me and command tactility are the material history and the shape of his encounters with other men; and as such these rings are the mimetic vehicle of a difference from "the body" which we men mime but which will never belong to us, except as the marks of endurance that it leaves on our bodies. Our mime brings us nothing outside of our relation in this place, and even here it buys only an appreciative glance, an evaluative touch, a drink perhaps.

With whom am I making pleasure if not with the mime itself (the other to each of us in this space)? The other here at the end of my fist is not any one man. The other is the group which already includes me. *The other is the technique* given me by the group that includes me. Public sex is a form of activism that makes space available for the next performance collective. *"You are queer visitor 55210,"* I learned when I visited Patrick's *way cool queer page* on December 20, 1996 (http://www.manzone.com/patrick). My visiting makes me queer. I am named, anointed, by the space I enter and, by entering, revise.

In a culture of masochism there is not a self prior to space and mapping its consciousness across space. In a culture of masochism self is a relatedness, not necessarily continuous, to the possible techniques of and paradigms for performance that have taken shape and been localized in various collective spaces—paradigms that precede the individual's entry into or use of those spaces. You too can be blindfolded and made to smell. I can require you to hold entire nosefuls of my sweat, urine, or semen. I am present in your nostrils, where you smell me. I have presence in the quivering of the hairs in your nose. My evanescence as a being is in your olfactory nerves, your cones and rods, your taste buds. I open you up to see myself on your retina. And then you blink. You reveal my flesh to me as you lick it. And then you swallow. I want to multiply the places where you can taste me. As we move from performance space to performance space we become different from the bodies we occupied elsewhere.

Top and bottom, exhibitionist and voyeur: these are merely tangential to whom I may be *in another place*. Their external structure imposed on my difference as an individual makes them powerful means for refusing the use of my private being in the public sphere. Top and bottom, exhibitionist and voyeur are in-body techniques, learned patiently and mastered over time, for submitting to a space that is not just an expression of myself. Public sex is my tactile relation to a space experienced through its collective spectacle: the leather fetish, the learned gesture, the downloaded image. A finger that belongs to no one and yet is in this space touches me. I maneuver that finger whenever I cross the threshold. And then I move on.

NOTES

1. See especially Freud, *Three Essays on the Theory of Sexuality*, pp. 63, 73, 76-78.

2. See Foucault, "Truth and Power," pp. 66-67; *The History of Sexuality, Volume I*, 105-114.

3. Of gays and the religious right, Patton writes: "both groups understand that they have radically different ideas of social space, one not easily adjudicated by the liberal pluralist fantasy of infinitely expandable space in which each minority gets its own 'private' sphere." Queer nationalism, she argues, invades public spaces "to signal that these territories have always been co-occupied" (Patton, "Public Enemy," p. 17).

4. Michel de Certeau showed that agents spatialize their world through their negotiations of normative or "proper" places. For agents, space is practiced place (Certeau, *The Practice of Everyday Life*, pp. xix, 35-37, 106-107, 117).

5. Bersani has described the orgasm as a momentary "shattering of the psychic structures themselves that are the precondition for the very establishment of a relation to others" (Bersani, "Is the Rectum a Grave?" pp. 215, 217).

6. Except for "live chat" situations, the Internet is asynchronous: any one segment of time or use of space is always available to other users in other segments of time (unlike a phone call, for example). I am not interested here in what is usually called "cybersex," those uses of the Internet that try to simulate situations of co-presence (live chat, for example).

WORKS CITED

Bersani, Leo. "Is the Rectum a Grave?" In *AIDS: Cultural Analysis, Cultural Activism*. Ed. Douglas Crimp. Cambridge, MA and London: MIT Press, 1988, pp. 197-222.

Certeau, Michel de. *The Practice of Everyday Life.* Trans. Steven Rendall. Berkeley, CA: University of California Press, 1984.

Foucault, Michel. *The History of Sexuality. Volume I: An Introduction.* Trans. Robert Hurley. New York: Pantheon, 1978.

————. "Truth and Power." In *The Foucault Reader.* Ed. Paul Rabinow. New York: Pantheon, 1984.

Freud, Sigmund. *Three Essays on the Theory of Sexuality.* Trans. and rev. ed. James Strachey. New York: Basic-HarperCollins, 1975.

Patton, Cindy. "Public Enemy: Fundamentalists in Your Face." *Voice Literary Supplement,* February 1993: 17-18.

Silverstein, Charles, and Edmund White. *The Joy of Gay Sex: An Intimate Guide for Gay Men to the Pleasures of a Gay Lifestyle.* New York: Simon and Schuster-Fireside, 1977.

Discourse: Dick

Simon Sheppard

Transgression? You want to talk transgression? Problem is, transgressions are a dime a dozen these days. You turn on Ricki or Geraldo or, God forbid, Jerry Springer, you see some transvestite storm-door salesman from Dubuque nattering on about how he just *loves* to lap up Mistress Ilsa's pee-pee from a dog dish. Then you channel surf over to MTV and there's Madonna (or *this* year's Madonna) in bondage yet again, the electrodes on her aging pussy wired to a field telephone being cranked up by Trent Reznor.[1] And for one momentous moment toward the end of the millennium, the entire world and CNN held its collective breath in rapt contemplation of the cum stains on Monica Lewinski's dress, jizz fetishism at its finest. Yawn . . . NEXT!

It's so hard to stay on the cutting edge, assuming there's even an edge left to cut. (I was just at our local theme park, where next to the souvenir T-shirts that said "I survived the Super-Coaster" were shirts that read "Been There, Pierced That." And they were marked down.) Sure, like all of you I've jacked off to Bataille and struggled through Foucault (who is, let's face it, so passé by now you might as well be reading Louisa May Fucking Alcott). And in some perverted way, I've taken it all *seriously*, even though Bataille, I hear, was an unpleasant drunk who would just as soon have puked on your shoes as looked at you. And Foucault? He must've been miffed when he had to take a break from getting beaten in some Folsom Street bathhouse long enough to write a book. So I guess he decided to punish *us*, make us suffer through his oblique, tortured, though no doubt meaningful-as-hell, prose.[2] Ooh-la-la, those French!

Et voilà, dear reader, in the spirit of jolly old postmodernity, you and I have already reached the point in this discourse where I'll interpolate the story of my very own performance piece. See, my pal Bill, the publisher of a local sex zine, periodically has me perform at these benefits he stages. So benefit time rolls around again and I need to come up with something to perform. But I'm really busy getting a couple of manuscripts out, and I'm trying to jump-start my first lesbian porn story, the tale of a Jewish communist dyke in prewar Berlin, just a tad pretentious. And as if I don't have enough on my plate, I'm in emotional turmoil, trying to get over a bottom boy with delusions of grandeur and a great big dick who made me tie him up and then broke my heart.[3]

Then one day I'm at the Queer Film Festival, watching this documentary about Nico. Remember Nico? She was this chanteuse with the Velvet Underground, later went on to be a solo act, doom-laden blonde Teutonic junkie . . . definitely ahead of her time. Anyway, there are all these people in the film and I get real melancholy because back when I was young, in the pre-postmodern era, I knew some of those people. (Like Jackson Browne, sensitive SoCal singer-songwriter who later became famous for allegedly beating up Darryl Hannah.[4])

I met a lot of that Warhol bunch, way back when I was crashing with my erstwhile roommate Fritz at the famous-but-tatty Chelsea Hotel. Fritz was doing the music for a Warhol film, *Women in Revolt*, which had something or other to do with Valerie Solanis, who's become something of a cottage industry herself these days.[5] I met Andy, and Candy Darling, who really *was* as gorgeous as they say, and Little Joe D'Allesandro, and Viva, and I'd already met Edie Sedgwick at some gallery opening or other. *Lots* of fabulous Warhol superstars, many of whom were, let's face it, dumber than a box of rocks. And Fritz's buddy Tony was directing Warhol's first (and blessedly only) stage play, eloquently titled *Pork*. Tony wanted me for a walk-on role, which as I recall involved wearing a silver-colored mask and standing around naked. But, to make a longish story shortish, I dutifully decided to go back to college, leaving the Factory and the legendary speed freaks and that whole scene far, far behind.

And later it turned out that David Bowie, at the very pinnacle of his trendiness, saw the play and loved it and all the people involved in *Pork* ended up working for *him*, helping staff his organization of set designers, costume designers, lighting designers, and other coked-out sycophants. Guess I missed out on *that* main chance.

So there I am, one afternoon many years later, sitting in the Castro Theatre, basically a seminobody who writes stroke stories, and I'm depressed, thinking two different but related thoughts. Thought one: If I had done things differently, I might have been a legend. Thought two: If I had done things differently, I might have been a *dead* legend.

Well, Nico comes to an untimely end, and so does the film. I leave the theatre, feeling more than a little mopey, and fortuitously run into my buddy Tim. When I first met Tim he was tied up, naked, modeling for a bondage class. I think it was the one on the quick-release rope harness, restrictive *and* convenient, just right for this modern age.[6] Later on I saw him in action at Leathernecks, which is this S/M party I help staff; that boy could take *some* punishment. And Tim, it turns out, is in point of fact not just a masochist but a major exhibitionist as well. Good boy!

So we're strolling down Castro Street when Tim says to me that he'd be really, really interested in helping me do a performance piece, particularly if it involves his taking off his clothes in front of a crowd. This gets me to thinking . . . I mean, it's hard to turn down an offer like that out of hand, but after all, I'm getting kind of a reputation as an erotic writer—"erotic writer," isn't *that* a pretentious bit of euphemism?[7] Face it, I'm a pornographer, maybe trying to be a literate, clever, cutting-edge pornographer, but smut is smut, God bless it. Writing *anything* has a certain cachet, though, unlike putting on male strip shows. So the question is: how am I going to incorporate Tim's generous offer to strip down and show his dick into a piece which is smart, and meaningful, and maybe funny to boot? I'm basically stymied.

I tell Tim I'll get back to him, but I never do. I start thinking maybe I'll take the easy way out and just read this fairy tale I wrote, which is actually pretty nice.[8] But not all that transgressive. Or maybe I'll just recite some art-fag poetry.[9] I'm at a loss.

A week or two later, I'm at this queer demonstration for or against something or other and I run into Tim again, and Tim tells me he's been thinking about doing a piece with me. Actually, he's been jerking off while fantasizing about jerking off in front of an audience. He says he really, really, really likes to show off.[10] And he tells me that basically he'll do anything I want him to. Which is pretty much what a top likes to hear. (Even though, as all you bottoms out there know—and God knows there are a *lot* of you—that sort of offer is usually a convenient fiction that collapses in the faintest breeze.)

Tim convinces me he'd love to help me out by beating off in front of a bunch of strangers, and he says he figures he can get it up, and I have faith in his judgment. And all this gets me interested in the possibilities again. Then this Big Idea comes to me: I can have Tim take his clothes off while I'm doing some kind of autobiographical rant. *See, self-exposure, get it?* I don't really like the Warhol schtick, though, I'm afraid it's going to be boring. So I'm sort of stuck with the transgressive stuff again. But I know that if I'm standing around talking about queer theory while a hot man is standing next to me playing with his dick, on one level it won't matter *what* the fuck I say. I could be talking about poststructuralism or reading the phone book. Right?

So OK, maybe there's an interesting idea here about word versus image. But I already deal in the endangered species of verbal communication . . . ask yourself, who the hell wants to make the effort to read a smutty story when you can just shove a cassette into the VCR? So why, oh why, should I show up language as the second-rate, highly mediated experience every writer knows in his/her heart of hearts it's become?[11] Maybe one of these days I should just surrender to the inevitable and give up the written word. I mean, while I was writing that last sentence, Kurt Cobain was on the CD player screaming, "You can't fire me 'cause I quit!"[12]

So the question is, am I comfortable subordinating my narrative to the very real real-time event of Tim trying (and succeeding admirably, I anticipate) to get it up and off? Let's face it, folks, whatever suspense arises, what the audience is going to be thinking isn't "What's Simon gonna say next?" It's "Is Tim actually gonna cum?" But the performance is coming up soon, and I've got to make some decisions. Fast.

So I call Bill and he says it's fine if Tim jacks off at his benefit, but I really should call Keith, since the show will be at his performance space. I leave a message for Keith, whom I kind of know but not really. He calls back a couple of hours later and says he thinks my message is really amusing, although I don't remember *trying* to be amusing. And, as I expected, he says that pretty much anything goes. I tell him what I plan to do, and that I hope it'll be sexy and witty. I add that I hope nobody in the audience will be offended (here I'm thinking "lesbian separatist," but then it's unlikely that too many lesbian separatists will show up for this particular event[13]). He's really nice and says that he hopes that Tim does an entertaining job of beating his meat. Actually, he says that he thinks the failure to be amusing is a much bigger crime than any sexual stuff he can think of. And when I hang up, I'm no longer worried about the sex stuff. I'm worried about the failure to be amusing. Which is pretty much what I worry about as an S/M top, too.

And then I realize that what I'd really like to do is make my part of the performance self-referential as hell. But I'm concerned that the piece will be too diffuse. Especially since it'll be obvious I'm reading the stuff, rather than it springing full-blown from my frontal lobes. I mean, I don't get laid a *lot* from my gigs, but I have tricked with at least a couple of guys who've seen me perform. And I'd rather that they think of me as a masterful S/M top with a razor-sharp wit than some insecure, garrulous schmuck with a flogger. So I sit down and write a text, this text, more or less. I mean the text that you would have read before Travers asked me to rewrite it for publication. (Yes, dear reader, for publication in this very book.) See, in the performance version, every so often I'd throw in an instruction to Tim: "Come up on stage, Tim." "Take your shirt off, Tim." "Pants, too." "Now your briefs." "You still have your socks on, Tim. Turn around, bend over, and take them off."[14]

Rehearsals are fun, especially synchronizing the text to Tim's erectile schedule. I'd make some cheesy joke about "performance anxiety," but on the night of the performance, all goes well. When I have Tim strip down, the audience becomes palpably more interested. When I tell Tim to jack off, he does so enthusiastically. The audience eats it up, metaphorically. Tim stays hard and happy. All this climaxes, as it were, when I say: "So I guess, in a funny way, I *have* achieved the arduous task of self-exposure. I'd like to mention the concept of metatexts here, but you guys are probably more interested in whether Tim here is going to blow his load, shoot his wad, let the baby batter flow. And it's that, the question of whether cum will flow, which invests so *many* sexual situations with more than a little anxiety, at least for us male-type guys. Which is exactly the moment of unknowability, the pivot point at which the written text ceases, must cease. *So how about it, Tim?"*

At this point, I put the text aside and turn to face Tim. To my great relief, things are going as planned; within thirty seconds flat, he ejaculates. Copiously. To thunderous applause.

That turned out to be the pinnacle of my performance-art career, but because the performance was so fucking site-specific, I figured that the text would never again see the light of day. But after I rewrote it for the printed page, D. Travers accepted it for inclusion in his book about pornography and performance art, tentatively titled *Strategic Sex*. Yes, dear reader, a project that metamorphosed into the volume you're now holding in your sweaty paws. Months later, the concept of the book had changed, and Travers wanted me to do yet another rewrite. Because he shamelessly flattered me,[15] I agreed to do the deed. His e-mail suggested changes I might make. Viz: "I mean, self-promotion is a valid aim of strategic sex. But there's something dare I say poignant about negotiating that in the current been-there-seen-that climate. Maybe you could write something personal, charting the same ideas in your life, using the Warhol gang, your perf with Tim, your stroke fiction-writing, and maybe public sex play as examples. If transgression is futile, what do you get out of bringing sex into public? Why do you do it?"

I felt like responding: "Because I'm a fucking show-off, that's why. Why do you think? Jeez, I thought that was abundantly clear from the text's subtext." But Travers' little note was so damn *nice* (I mean: "But there's something dare I say poignant . . ." Who among us can resist the use of "dare I say"?) that I restrained myself.

But I will say it. I do this stuff because I'm a fucking show-off, that's why. A smart-ass show-off.[16]

And because sex, especially kinky sex, isn't just performance art. It's showbiz.

Fucking showbiz. Which there is no fucking business like.

So let's go on with the show.

NOTES

1. See Tiffany Zero, "Nine-Inch Nails and the Search for Sacred Space," *The Journal of Sub-Pop Literacy* 6(9) (May, 1996): 12-24. "Clearly, if Madonna

hadn't existed, the demands of postmodernism would have required that she be invented. Perhaps she was."

2. Maurice "Spike" McGuire, *Michel Foucault As I Knew and Fisted Him* (Vienna: Doppelgänger Press, 1996). It's a cliché to go on about how the French think Jerry Lewis is a great intellectual, but I doubt that even Lewis himself could make it through *A History of Sexuality, Part 1* and keep a straight face.

3. See Simon Sheppard, "He Made Me Tie Him Up and Then He Broke My Heart," in *Whiny Tops*, Pat Califia, ed. (San Francisco: Overdetermined Publishers, 1996), pp. 138-155.

4. I got to know Jackson shortly after he and Nico broke up, actually roomed with him for a while on the Lower East Side, back when Soho was just another slum. Once watched him take a bath in one of those Avenue C kitchen-sink-cum-bathtub arrangements. Don't remember his dick, though. . . .

5. Lyzz Argot-Manwomyn, "Valerie Solanis: A Loony Loser and the Creation of a Myth," *Hopelessly Trendy Magazine* (May, 1996): 45-48. "I mean, she shot somebody, she was a crazy scuzzball who tried to kill somebody famous. And now they're making *movies* about her, for Chrissakes. We should all be so lucky." A minority view, to be sure, but a trenchant one.

6. See Jacques Rien, "Bondage in Theory and Theory," *Le Journal de Plus Ça Change* 6/9 (Mai, 1996): 3-22. "The top's gaze is the gaze of God in a universe where God does not exist."

7. See Camille Faux, " 'Pornographer' or 'Erotic Writer': What the Fuck's the Difference?," *The Journal of Newfangled Language* 6(9) (May, 1996): 69.

8. Plug: Simon Sheppard, "The Ugly Duckling," in *Happily Ever After: Fairy Tales for Men*, Michael Ford, ed. (New York: Richard Kasak Books, 1996), pp. 91-97. Really.

9. Simon Sheppard, "Deconstruct THIS, Motherfucker," *The Harvard Review of Poetry* (May, 1996): 143.

10. Like I don't already know that—every time I've seen him at a play party, he's been stark naked and dripping.

11. CompuServe 36788.5965.342218,098, "The Book as Fetish Object," *E-mailer Monthly* 2.4 (May, 1996): 8-11.

12. Poor Kurt.

13. But see the manifesto by Andrea MacKinnon, "We'll Go Where We're Not Welcome and Then Complain That Everyone Resents Us," in *Hairy Legs* (May, 1996): 10.

14. A particularly felicitous moment, as in bending over he offers up his ass to the collective gaze of the audience, deconstructing his crack, as it were.

15. And because, let's face it, D. Travers Scott is "my type": tall, skinny, young, cute. And willing to publish my stuff.

16. See· *The Neo-Tribal Review of Culture*, May 1996. This special issue, "Self-Indulgence: Art Form for Our Time," is the source of many of the ideas I stole for this piece. Shamelessly.

Annabel's Cookies

Karen Green

It was early in 1994, right around the same time that Annabel's Cookies started practicing, that someone told me if I were a boy I would have women, "girls," mad at me all the time. And though I am here, trying to stand at my own defense, I realize it doesn't matter if I am a boy or not. Girls still get mad at me all the time. And I don't doubt that on some level, I am a boy.

And you know what? It's tough being the only boy in Annabel's Cookies. Four other busty and scantily clad women made up the band with me, the boy, playing drums.

Lots of times at shows one or two of the girls would come back to my kit during a song and shake their tits at me. This was to acknowledge my presence because I am often so small behind the drums I can't be seen.

I don't mind them giggling at me so much during the show, it being an act and all. But sometimes the temptation wouldn't stop. Usually, we'd all go out and drink ourselves sick after the show, and then all four of them would taunt and flirt with me. I'll admit I liked it, but I also got very bored and insecure because not one of these girls ever came home with me.

One night, we were playing at a club called Love Thy Neighbor. After the show, a really cute girl named Abbey came up to me and was giving me some lecture on art when I felt someone blow in my ear. Of course it was one of the Cookies, and she had that "fuck me now, baby" look, as if she meant it. A part of me started smoldering while another part fumed. Abbey said, "I didn't know you had a girlfriend."

"I don't," I said, perhaps jerkily. "This is Colleen, she's in my band, Annabel's Cookies," I blurt as I lean over into her ear. I realized then that the spit from my beer sip had hit Abbey in the ear canal and remorse set in. She looked annoyed.

I smiled and laughed. "Oh, come on baby, really. Colleen, tell her."

"Hey," Colleen began. "I thought you were coming home with me tonight."

Sabotage. My mouth dropped, and this wasn't the first time. Abbey huffed and walked away. Colleen stood there laughing. "What do you need a cunt like that for? You know what your problem is? You always set yourself up so you can't get what you want. And I've watched you do it a thousand times. You like being hurt."

My friend turned a little to her left, trying to avoid my piercing glance. But I was ready for her tonight. "Well, who the fuck are you to tell me how to live my life? If I want to keep not getting what I want, I will. Fuck you." I slammed my beer down on the bar mumbling, I'll never play with them again.

Then, it was like some bizarre yet touching flinch of karma intervened. I bumped into this beautiful and wholesome blond-haired woman I'd met through one of the band members on my way out the door. Her name was Sidney. I smiled and apologized for almost ransacking her, and she smiled, winked eyelashes, and told me she liked being that close to me. I asked her if she wanted a beer, she accepted, and we sat and chatted briefly. Tana came up to us and asked me if I knew where some piece of equipment had been stored and I blanched and told her I was too messy to think. My pretty blond girl didn't seem to mind, though, so I asked her to come to the rest room with me. She acquiesced.

As soon as we got in a stall she tried kissing me. I laughed and pushed her away, turned her around and pressed her up against the wall. I pulled her skirt up over her hips and pulled her soft white cotton panties down just below her ass.

"What?" She was startled by my aggressiveness.

"Shhh, baby, it's okay. I'm just going to take you in the ass."

"But . . ."

I wasn't psyched that she was hesitant, it tore at me immediately. I caressed her ass, ran my hand between the cheeks and into her hot wet pussy. Just as my fingers slid inside her cunt, I heard the bathroom door open and some catty girls talking.

"Don't you think Johnny should just go and tell his girlfriend that he wants to be with me and get it over with? I mean, what's the big deal; it's just sex."

She went into the stall next to us, but the conversation continued while she peed.

"Yeah, well, he's a wimp you know. I read some stuff in his diary the other day and all he did was bitch about people and mope about how lame his life is. Pretty boring."

"Really. He seems so hip and on fire. Did he show it to you or something?"

"Uh, no, I just found it in the kitchen. You know, you know that thing, possession is nine tenths of the law. Plus, it's my house."

The door to the stall opened. "I don't think God would approve, you know."

"Fuck that, I don't believe in bullshit like God. Do you?"

The door to the bathroom opened and the two girls left. I moved my hand inside the blond and pushed my thumb into her asshole. I was holding her still and we had nearly stopped breathing with the interruption. I unzipped my pants and started to pull out my dick when the bathroom door opened again.

"Hey, drummer girl, you in here? I know you're masturbating in that stall, you drunken shit, come on, we're leaving." It was Tana.

I didn't move. I could feel every footstep of Tana's as she slowly approached the stall. She banged on the door hard and then smashed it open. I'd had enough preparation time to pull up the girl's undies and zip my fly so the intrusion lacked the potential never-live-down embarrassment it possessed.

"*Jeez*," said Tana. "They get younger every time."

"Fuck you," and I pushed her against the sink. "Maybe if you weren't such a mean bitch, you'd get laid by some sexy sixteen-year-old, too." I left the bathroom, blond in tow, and grabbed my coat.

"Oh, no," said Darcy, "you're not bringing her home with us. You gotta put your shit away. What do we look like here? Slaves?"

The rest of the night was a blur. My blond was too rattled to continue this journey and I was in no state of mind to provide comfort. I flopped into the back of the van and stretched out. Darcy got in back with me and tried to lay near me. I pulled myself tight inside my body and went to sleep.

Moby Dick in the China Sea:
Great White Pornography in Taiwan

R. R. Katz

As a student of Chinese culture and an observer of pornography from age ten (when I became enthralled by R. Crumb's big-legged women in *Zap Comics*), a search for pornography was an unavoidable theme of my travels in Taiwan. Taiwan is an island reservoir of unbridled capitalism and traditional Chinese culture. The first time I went there, in the early 1980s, the island was still under martial law and many aspects of communication and expression, including arts and performance, were strictly censored. Any foreigner entering the country at that time had the experience of having their bags emptied, their magazines leafed through and their videos viewed. The Taiwan customs agents had to be thorough, lest any pornography or communist influence from the licentious West should seep through the cracks and pollute the Confucian ideals that the older generation of autocrats in Taiwan were trying to enforce. The followers of the corrupt Nationalist government of Chiang Kai Shek feared nothing more than an impulsive and freedom-loving populace. Apparently, pornography was a sure sign of societal problems in their eyes.

Taiwan's borders were quite porous ten years ago when I first went there and, when it comes to pornography, still are. Taiwan has its own pornography industry that flourishes. Confucian strictures can bring guilt (and how could the pornography industry survive without lots of delicious guilt on the part of the consumer?), but Chinese guilt can't compare to the eternity rotting in Hell that Christian countries promise to moral transgressors. The first impression one gets in Taipei is that of a chaste city; a city without sexual advertising or risqué TV programming. But any foreigner who turns off the main streets or strolls around at night discovers that pornography is thriving and generally ignored by the authorities.

My first local movie was typical of the soft-core porn popular in Taiwan and Hong Kong. I selected the movie because of a poster showing Chinese women striking suggestive poses in hot pants while holding firearms. The movie turned out to be about a group of female vigilantes who had been abused by men and who took their revenge by attacking those male dregs of society. The women were usually tortured a bit first and ended up doing their attacking in their underwear. The mission of these women was to render men incapable of ever abusing women again. During the climactic showdown at the end of the movie, the mostly male audience cackled with delight when the women cornered a man at night in a park and used a flamethrower to render his genitals harmless. There was no full nudity in this movie and hardly any bad language, mostly just kung fu fighting, rape, and off-screen sexual mutilation. The next day, images of the movie still in my mind, I crowded onto a bus full of innocent, sweet-looking high school girls in uniform. I arrived at the language school that I was attending and a German student happened to show me an article about a sexual abnormality which Asian males suffered from. The abnormal men feared that their penises were shrinking into their bodies and as a result tugged on themselves, sometimes causing damage. It made me think of yesterday's movie viewers. Did they go home and pull on their penises with images of mutilation fresh in their minds?

Many quotes from the Confucian *Analects* promote the idea of a strict moral code and a hierarchy with autocratic rulers and subservient subjects. This ingrained philosophy is what Chinese totalitarian leaders through the centuries have leaned on to maintain power. Other quotes from the *Analects* say in no uncertain terms that women and eunuchs were one cause of a man's fall from morality. Furthermore, according to the Confucian domino theory, once one man succumbed to licentiousness a chain of events was set off and soon the whole nation would fall into moral decay and collapse. This theory is not unlike theories we now hear in the United States from the religious right: outlawing behavior that they find distasteful, such as graphic song lyrics, will help solve societal problems. Confucius went on to describe the harm that improper music or entertainment could cause. Confucius believed that good men only listened to the uplifting music and dance of the ancient sages.

Xiao Mei (Little Rose) was my first girlfriend in Taiwan. Although Chinese girls were said to be shy and demure, I found the girls in Taiwan and mainland China quite aggressive and curious when it came to foreign men. It didn't take Xiao Mei long to introduce sex into our relationship and she did it in a curious manner. She showed me a small Taiwanese porno magazine that had one blurry black and white photo of a Caucasian male with an extremely long, semi-flaccid penis hanging almost down to his knee. I discovered in my conversation with Chinese of both sexes that Americans were looked upon by them as horny, well-endowed, sexual animals. The image that many Taiwanese had of American women being easy and of the American males having large dicks reminded me of white people's stereotypes of African Americans back home. The joke among American males in Taiwan when it came to eager Chinese females was that they were searching for Moby Dick: the Great White Whale.

At the same time Confucianism took hold in China as the dominant philosophy, a rich culture of pornography developed that reveled in mocking the conservatism of the rigid Confucian moral code. It was a classic Taoist balance in which the more people (in this case Confucianists) struggled against improper behavior, the more an ever-bigger void was created that had to be filled by exactly the thing the people in charge were trying to do away with.

A young man whom I was tutoring in English decided to take me to one of Taipei's more famous strip joints. It was in the seedy, old part of Taipei behind the Dragon Mountain Temple. Dragon Mountain was a great old temple smelling of incense and filled with dank, calming spirituality. The streets behind the temple were infamous for having every kind of sexual commerce imaginable. The best-known street, called Snake Alley, was a common stop for the heartier tourists who visited Taiwan. Snakes writhing in cages were auctioned off almost exclusively to male customers. The more venomous the snake, the more expensive it was. The snakes were hung up by the neck and slit down their undersides so that a clear liquid could be squeezed out of a sack midway down their still-writhing bodies. The liquid was squeezed into a cup of brandy and the customer would gulp it down and move on. The snake liquid was used by men because they believed it enhanced their sexual prowess. The odd thing to me was that it was used by the Chinese men before they went to see the prostitutes who plied their trade farther down Snake Alley. Why was it important to impress a prostitute with one's sexual prowess?

The brothels of Snake Alley were crammed together in very narrow alleyways. That warm night as I approached the area, stale sexual smells hung thick in the air. As potential customers walked down the alleys, many very young girls came up and grabbed and tugged on them. The men pretended that they didn't really want to visit prostitutes and it only came about because the sex-crazed prostitutes forced them into the dens of iniquity. In front of me a short, pudgy, balding man was smiling and putting up a bit of a struggle as four girls picked him up and moved him bodily into their shabby, wooden place of business.

My destination that night was not a brothel, it was an X-rated performance. We walked through a maze of alleys, up some stairs of an unmarked building and into a theater that was surprisingly elegant in its decoration. There were chandeliers, candles on the tables, and a stage resplendent with a shimmering satin curtain. My curiosity was piqued. I had heard Spalding Gray's monologue about Thai bar girls who shot bananas out of their vaginas and I wanted to be similarly wowed.

What came out on stage were a half-dozen Western women who looked like they had seen a few too many tours of duty. They were for the most part overweight with lots of flaccid skin and I suppose had larger breasts than most Chinese women. The six women, coincidentally, had the exact same platinum-blonde hair color. Basically, these women were quite unattractive in my eyes; they looked like miserable, alcoholic, divorced mothers from Florida. How they ended up in G-strings in this back-alley establishment in Taiwan was beyond me. They performed typical, topless striptease routines to the extent the physical limitations would allow. They did this individually and then in groups. The audience loved them. Some of them called out in English, "Good, sexy!" No one tried to get particularly close to the women; the audience was transfixed as if they sat before shimmering goddesses.

My student wanted to rave about the show with me but soon saw I wasn't nearly as enthusiastic. "You really thought that those girls were great?"

"American girls sexy. Chinese girls not so good. Don't like sex."

That hadn't been my experience but maybe I was just projecting my own equally unreal fantasies of the exotic oriental sex goddess schooled in the ancient secrets of lovemaking on the Chinese girls I had met.

I stayed in Taiwan two more years, studying the language, painting, and calligraphy. By the end of the two years, I had become acculturated to the point that Chinese women no longer aroused my fantasies and those loose, heavy-mammaried American women started looking better and better. The night before I left Taiwan I was on a crowded bus to northern Taipei. It took a few moments before I realized a mousy little Chinese woman who appeared to be in her thirties was rubbing her vagina against my hand as I grasped the back of a seat. I became interested and did not try to withdraw my hand. It took a few more moments for me to realize that several riders were intently watching our little pornographic exhibition. Suddenly the woman darted toward the front of the bus. I tried to follow her off but she obviously wanted nothing more to do with me. She got off in the theater district. The last I saw of her, she darted into a theater behind a large billboard showing James Bond pointing a gun right between some shapely, bare legs. It was a hand-painted billboard and, as often happened with Chinese paintings of Americans, features like the nose were exaggerated to look almost comical. The legs were large and heavy to the point of looking matronly. A huge crowd was gathered, eager for the entertainment the billboard promised.

White Skinhead
Seeks Black Submissives

Jayson Marston

White Skinhead seeks black submissives to panty train and service my boots. You will be trained to lick and suck until I'm happy. Respond now.

"Hi. Now that you decided I'm going to be your master, leave your number and we'll have some fun."

"Racist motherfucker." Click.

"You are exactly the sick type of individual that gives gay people a bad name and. . . ." Beep.

"What, you leather fags don't get enough oppression from the world. . . ."

"Yeah, I saw your ad and would like to get together. Call me. . . ."

"Yeah. Hi . . . oh about six feet . . . yeah, I think we'll have fun . . . Really? People wasted a dollar ninety-nine a minute to leave you stupid messages? . . . Yeah, I'll be over tomorrow."

"On your knees you little bitch," I bark as soon as I close the door to my bedroom. He drops to his knees and looks down at the ground. My boots are polished to a shine as bright as black glass. My jeans are rolled just right. They show off my boots and make him see the power I have over him. My torso is covered by a white tank top and crossed by my white braces. I look down at him and spit in his black face. "Strip!" He pulls off his clothes and piles them on the floor next to him. I walk over to the closet and grab a dress and wig out of the box on the floor. I toss them over to him and tell him to dress like that pretty bitch he is. He pulls the dress over his gym-worked frame and pulls the wig over his short dreadlocks. "There. Now, you little slut. Now you look like the bitch I want to fuck." I grab him by the back of the neck and stand her up in front of the mirror on the back of my door. "Now look at you; you're just a little fucking whore. I oughta turn you out and make some fucking money off yer holes." I put my arm around her head. In the mirror my arm is Aryan white interrupted only by tattoos and black curly wig hair. I start working my fingers in her mouth and watch as my fingers disappear past her thick lips. "I'm gonna teach you what evil is."

I push her by her face to a kneeling position on the floor. "Don't move." I pull a chair from the corner of the room and put it right in front of the mirror. "Now you're gonna lick these skinhead boots clean." I push her down and she's face to face with the mirror. I take a seat and put one boot in front of her and the other up under her dress. "Now clean them boots off." She opens her mouth and in the mirror I see her tongue start working the toe of my boot. I push the toe of my other boot up against her asshole. She starts to squirm on it and my dick starts to crowd my jeans. "Yeah, that's right, lick that boot, you little nigger bitch. You like that, don't ya?" She starts to whimper and grind her hole harder into my boot. "All right, that's enough. Now get up." She stands up and her stiff cock makes a tent in the front of her dress. I stand up and look into her face. Her brown eyes look away from my blue. I reach down and grab her cock. "You're not the lady you look to be. You're just a trannie slut aren't you?" She begins to speak and I cut that short with a slap that brings forth some tears. "Aww, a little crybaby, aren't ya? Well too fucking bad. No one forced you here, and now you're not leaving till I'm done with you." I grab the back of her neck and lick her face from chin to forehead, leaving a wet streak down the middle. I'm the violator and she's my hot piece of snatch. I turn her and push her belly down in front of the mirror. "Now you're gonna watch me hump your black ass and you're gonna like it so much that you'll scream for me to stop." With one hand I pull the tank top off over my head. I reach down and undo the fly of my jeans. I push her dress up and start working her hole with my greased-up fingers.

She reaches down and pushes her cock back so that it will also get some of my attention. I grease her hole up and put on a rubber. "OK bitch, when I fuck you, I want to hear your black ass holler." I stick it in her and begin to pump away. I grab her chin and make her watch her ass getting fucked by skinhead dick. In the mirror my face gets red and my mouth opens in a yell. I roll off her and sit on the edge of the bed. I toss the spent latex into a bag near my bed. She comes around to the bed and lies down on the floor. She starts licking my boot and jerking off under her dress. Her face grimaces and she pulls her dick faster. She blows her load and shakes twice. "You made a mess of that dress." "Yeah, and I got drool all over your boots." She gets up and grabs my shirt off the floor. Before I can reach out and grab the shirt she's wiped her load off with it. "Bitch !" She laughs and throws it at my head. I get up and put my arms around her. I unzip the dress and it falls onto the ground. Then I grab the wig and drop it on the floor. I kiss him on the neck and take his hand. I lead him into the bathroom and run the shower. After we wash up and get dressed I walk him to the door. I give him a kiss good-bye and tell him to call me again.

Interview with a Metamorphosexual

Marti Hohmann with Annie Sprinkle

Marti Hohmann: Some of the techniques you describe in your show and teach in your workshops include breath orgasm, nongenital sex, and connecting with the sexual energy in the sky, mud, and trees. How are these techniques revolutionary?

Annie Sprinkle: Breath orgasm is not revolutionary; it's a form of energy orgasm, which is an ancient technique, just as yoga is an ancient technique. It's simply being rediscovered and becoming popular.

I first became aware of it when I was with a group taking a workshop with Harley Swiftdeer. I was writing an article for *Penthouse Forum*. They sent me to Harley's workshop, which I had wanted to go to anyway. At the end of the workshop, he said, "Now we're going to do the fire-breath orgasm." There was a group of people there who had been studying with Harley for a while. His wife and one of his assistants lay down on the floor and started breathing through the chakras (the breathing brings sexual energy up through the body). Eventually they had these very intense orgasms, and I thought, "This is incredible; I have to learn how to do this." At first you think, "This can't be real," because it goes against the grain of everything you've been taught, but I could see and feel that they were having orgasms.

The demonstration lasted about twenty minutes, and then Harley said, "Now we're all going to do it." We got on the floor in the shape of a wagon wheel, with everyone's head toward the center, and we all started breathing deeply. Many of the people already knew how to do it. This was happening in Michigan, of all places; regular folks were breathing themselves into incredible orgasmic experiences. Some of them were screaming and crying. There were women there who were much more sexually advanced than I was, and I'd been around the block.

I went back to New York, but no one there knew much about it. I got a copy of Harley Swiftdeer's manual and started practicing, but I wasn't getting it. I taught the technique to several friends, even though I couldn't do it. I showed my Tantra teacher how to do it, and she got it. Then I found out that another Tantra teacher named Kutira taught something called "the wave." To do the wave, you breathe and undulate while standing until you have an energy orgasm. I invited her to my house and I presented an evening with friends. That night I saw a few more energy orgasms.

I used to go to the park and practice. During the first year, I would start crying every time I did it. The energy would come up to my heart and then hit a block, and I would cry. The second year, the block was in my throat, so I would choke: I even threw up a couple of times. Finally I started getting it. It took me three years, but eventually I had several huge energy orgasms. If you breathe for an hour and really relax, you feel like you're plugged into the wall. It's extremely electric, a very deep orgasm, and definitely a spiritual experience. There are many levels of orgasm: sometimes light ones, but also heavy-duty, electric ones.

I've seen other people do it much better than I can do it now. I saw a guy who had been practicing for twelve years—he had done it every day. He had the most amazing orgasm I've ever seen. It's becoming quite popular because it's an incredible technique, which is very good for your health and emotional well-being. Energy orgasms aren't always sexual; sometimes they are, but sometimes they're not.

Marti: What is a nonsexual orgasm?

Annie: It feels like a big release of energy. First there's a buildup of energy; then at a certain point it releases throughout the body. The energy is not in your genitals; it could be in your heart or throat, for example. An analogy might be to a cry or a sneeze, or a good hard laugh. Think of how wonderful you feel when you've been laughing hysterically, and then you stop; you feel good, but the feeling is not in your pussy. Try to imagine you could have a laugh in your pussy, then imagine its opposite: an energy orgasm is like having an orgasm in your laughter. There are different kinds: little waves or major releases.

Marti: In *Vice Versa: Bisexuality and the Eroticism of Everyday Life*, Marjorie Garber notes that transgression is often used to represent the erotic in Western culture.[1] Is the energy orgasm transgressive sex?

Annie: Yes, in that you're opening yourself up to the energy available in the universe. You're opening your mind to all its possibilities. Human beings are capable of meditating nude in the snow and melting the snow. Yogis do all kinds of amazing things. An energy orgasm is much easier, comparatively speaking.

Marti: Does the change in your work have political implications?

Annie: It certainly has safe-sex implications and feminist implications. When you are sexually knowledgeable, you open yourself up to a tremendous source of power. The personal becomes political, especially because energy orgasm is healing. If we could use orgasm to become healthier, happier, stronger and more emotionally well-balanced, we could take over the world.

A wise gay man once said, "As I receive pleasure, so the whole universe receives pleasure through me." That's one of my favorite quotes, and it has obviously broader political implications.

Marti: As a performance mode, there are ways in which the shift toward energy orgasm might be interpreted as less risky than your previous work. There's no nudity involved, for example, and you don't use sex toys.

Annie: It seems much more risky to me.

Marti: Because it makes you more vulnerable?

Annie: You can't always control an energy orgasm; sometimes it will happen, but other times it won't. Taking a risk is performing in front of three hundred people who expect to see an energy orgasm, when you know you might not have one. Talk about performance anxiety!

Marti: But pornography is a genre most audiences immediately understand as transgressive. Given today's political climate, the presentation of an orgasm which doesn't involve nudity or genital contact might seem like appeasement or avoidance.

Annie: It's a very advanced type of orgasm, though. You have to have a certain level of knowledge and awareness to do it. It's more interesting to have an orgasm without touching because it's more rare.

Marti: You're also theorizing a different relationship to the body.

Annie: I'm putting myself more on the line, especially because 95 percent of the people in the audience don't believe an energy orgasm is possible. I'm going against everything they've been taught. I have to hope they can get a sense of what energy is about. I'm affected by other people's energy, so I'm trusting my audience to be wise and mature.

Marti: You seem to address matters of the heart more in your recent work. At your Boston show in July of '95, when asked what you would do differently if given the chance to remake your career, you said, "I'd show real love between people and real tenderness. I'm not into the rough stuff anymore because I don't want to hurt anyone."

Annie: I used to get fucked really hard. It would turn me on. But what gives us an orgasm isn't always necessarily good for us. Now I like nurturing, tenderness, gentleness, caring, and softness. Sounds kinky, I know. But I believe most of us want that on a deeper level.

Marti: You've indicated that *Post-Modern Pin-Ups: Pleasure Activist Playing Cards,*[2] which features sex activists and performers like Kat Sunlove, Dolores French, Susie Bright, Candida Royalle, and Fanny Fatale, is your last project involving pinups. Why have you decided to leave that form behind?

Annie: I'm very proud of the playing cards, which I think are great for men and women, but my aesthetic has changed. With pinups, the focus is on costumes, lingerie, and makeup, and they depend on a certain kind of lustiness, a certain cuteness. For the most part they represent a heterosexual aesthetic which is very often patriarchal and sometimes misogynistic. I had fun with this aesthetic: I wanted to be Bettie Page; I wanted to be a *Playboy* model; I wanted to look like a movie star. Then I realized that anyone can do that with the right costumes, lighting, and makeup.

Now I'm interested in creating a mood; I like seeing women in more powerful postures. Pinups can portray a powerful woman, but ultimately the model is vulnerable, submissive, and available. Shit, I sound like the people I used to debate against!

Marti: But the pleasure-activist pinups are different. In *This Sex Which Is Not One*, Luce Irigaray talks about mimicry, which she defines as knowing how to manipulate a certain "language" (in this case, the language of the sex-fashion system) in order to formulate a sociopolitical critique.[3] I think she means that it can be useful to learn how to use the traditional signifiers of sex in order to have a sense of one's mastery in the sexual playground. The hard part, of course, is figuring out where the edge is: knowing when you're wearing the stiletto heels because you want to and not because someone else wants you to.

Annie: This is something many of us struggle with. Many women like sexy clothing but don't like what it stands for. I used to be very pro-high heels, for example, and people would question me about that from different perspectives. Now I'm starting to understand what they were talking about. My initial response had been, "They're only shoes. What does that have to do with anything?" But I think there is a connection to a larger picture. There are deeper issues.

Marti: In the playing cards, your models seem very much in control of their own representations. The same might be said of "Anatomy of a Pin-Up Photo," which appears in *Post-Porn Modernist*.[4] You deconstruct the pinup's sexuality by detailing exactly how such representations are generated, but then you go one step further and add, "In spite of it all, I'm sexually excited and feeling great."

Annie: My instincts have been good. I'm glad I don't get stuck in anything too much. I like changing. It's exciting. Sometimes I think I've come to the end of the road and I had better find some subject matter besides sex, but then all of a sudden I get new inspiration.

Marti: How do you connect yourself to the larger community of sex-positive women?

Annie: I see myself as one of the few women who has been involved in mainstream sex work and porn who is working in the art world now. There are people in art who have gone the other direction somewhat. Some of my friends have become much more commercial than I have. There are many different genres of sexually explicit material, and I'm certainly more interested in the more arty kind, which is more eclectic, experimental, and off-the-wall. That's where I'm at my best and am happiest.

Marti: But what about the HBO specials?

Annie: I've worked with HBO three times now. They did a special on my workshop, *Sluts and Goddesses*, and a segment on a show called *Real Sex.* I just finished shooting an hour-long special on the *Pleasure Activist Playing Cards* and the women in them. HBO calls for a very mainstream perspective, but they actually have done a fairly good job of homogenizing what I do.

Marti: What happens when Annie Sprinkle plays a mainstream audience?

Annie: Now I get recognized at the airport, the library, McDonald's. Regular folks see HBO, whereas when I perform in an art venue the audience is more specific. I like the art audience the best: I like where they're at, and I feel seen and understood there.

Marti: Perhaps it's exciting, though, to know you're being seen by people who otherwise would never have been exposed to your work.

Annie: I would love to be mainstream, but my natural talents do not lie there. For example, if I tried to do mainstream burlesque now, it wouldn't work. I'd love to be a Las Vegas showgirl; I'd love to be a fabulous stripper. I'd love to be a fabulous porn star, but that's not where I belong anymore. I don't look, think, or act the part. I'd rebel like hell.

Marti: One change you've mentioned in your work has been moving from fantasy (as Annie) to meditation (as Anya). In the interview in *Voices from the Edge*, you suggest that as Anya, you prefer to meditate rather than fantasize.[5]

Annie: Fantasizing uses your imagination; meditating is letting go of your thoughts or being a witness to your thoughts. It's opening up and relaxing rather than working the mind.

Marti: Does that mean you're less interested in representations of fantasy life, like erotica?

Annie: I'm still interested in erotica. I love Susie Bright's book about the history of lesbian photography [*Nothing but the Girl: The Blatant Lesbian Image*[6]] because it's so hot and sexy. Personally I never use the word "fantasy" because it implies something that isn't real or isn't tangible. Instead of "fantasy," I prefer "living one's desires" or "being sexually creative." Fantasy, to me, is something that certain guys do—guys who could never have or do what they desire.

These days I'm most interested in the eroticism of truth. In my workshop, for example, I try not to tell other people how to be. I want to get at the heart of what they feel, in the eroticism of their truth, of their reality.

Different things are erotic to me than five or ten years ago. Sometimes even the opposite things are erotic to me, which is surprising. Women, for example, are now sexy to me. A leather garter belt and bra used to turn me on, but now I just think they look old-fashioned and silly. What excites me is just a naked woman, especially if she has lots of pubic hair. That's surprising, too, because I used to think a shaved pussy was erotic. I kept mine shaved for years. Now I let it all grow.

Marti: It sounds like you've put away the props.

Annie: Except for my vibrator.

Marti: No doubt there's also something about change which is itself arousing.

Annie: Yes, I would say so. But I have to be careful not to think I've got my finger on the pulse all the time. I still do the *Sluts and Goddesses* workshop, for example, and some women adore the slut costumes, whereas I'm bored with them. I have to remember that everyone's at a different place in their lives.

Marti: Since participants in your workshops often tell their sexual life stories, can you elaborate on the connection between autobiography and performance?

Annie: Of course autobiography is part of the tradition of performance art. To me, that's why performance art is such a great outlet.

Marti: But beginning with Rousseau, or in a more oblique way, even with St. Augustine, the genre of autobiography has often entailed sexual confession. Very often a sexual truth forms a crucial part of the telling of one's life story.

Annie: There's certainly an eroticism in telling your life story. It's like making love with your audience.

Marti: It sounds as if you will be encouraging women to reconsider ecstasy in its larger sense, perhaps even to reclaim it and remake it for themselves. Is there such a thing as feminist ecstasy?

Annie: What do you mean?

Marti: It's what I imagine when I see your work. I suppose I mean an apex of pleasure which is necessarily woman-centered and political.

Annie: I don't think ecstasy has a gender; I also don't think ecstasy has to be sexual. I go into ecstasy after jogging two miles. When I stop and rest, I like to put my feet in the water and watch the birds fly. It's quiet and still. For me ecstasy is definitely linked to spirituality.

Marti: You seem to offer people an accessible ecstasy—an ecstasy which must be worked at, but which is nonetheless available.

Annie: Yes. Ecstasy is available for the asking. It's a choice. It can be manifested by creating a simple chemical reaction in the body. Just open your heart and your mind, and remember how ecstasy feels, and it's there.

NOTES

1. Garber, Marjorie. *Vice Versa: Bisexuality and the Eroticism of Everyday Life.* New York: Simon and Schuster, 1995.

2. Gates, Katherine, ed. *Post-Modern Pin-Ups: Pleasure Activist Playing Cards.* Richmond, VA: Gates of Heck, 1995.

3. Irigaray, Luce. *This Sex Which Is Not One,* Catherine Porter with Carolyn Burke, Trans. Ithaca, NY: Cornell University Press, 1985.

4. Sprinkle, Annie. *Post-Porn Modernist: My 25 Years As a Multi-Media Whore.* San Francisco: Cleis Press, 1998.

5. *Voices from the Edge: Conversations with Jerry Garcia, Ram Dass, Annie Sprinkle, Matthew Fox, Jaron Lanier and Others.* Interviews by David Brown and Rebecca McClen Novick. Freedom, CA: Crossing Press, 1995.

6. Bright, Susie and Posner, Jill, eds. *Nothing But the Girl: The Blatant Lesbian Image.* New York: Freedom Editions, 1996.

Porno-formance:
Some Notes on Sex As Art

Carol Queen

If this culture were not so over-the-top loco about sex, no one would consider problematizing (or defending) art with sexual content. But we're lunatic, schizo, downright mad. So sex-and-body art occupies a category of its own, usually selling out performance houses but out in the cold when it comes to reliable sources of funding and real legitimacy.

As an artist who deals with sex and the eroticized body in every medium in which I work, I take this very personally. As a trained sexologist, I view it as a symptom of a deep cultural ambivalence: audiences that balk and titter at sexual themes and content think nothing of letting sexual innuendo and their own (often unacknowledged) erotic hunger drive their purchasing decisions, since suggestive advertising is this country's greatest source of sexual entertainment.

I take it personally not so much because I want easier access to grant money—it has scarcely occurred to me to apply for any, because I read the papers, you see, and I know Jesse Helms would be right up my keister if I tried to get my hands on any taxpayer dollars. Rather, I take it personally because being constrained to the artistic version of the Tenderloin District means that I have a limited ability to explore the issues that are important to me—sexual issues —in the presence of the mainstream public, the audience that needs most to hear what I have to say.

Every performance artist burns a high-octane mixture of ego and issue: exhibitionism and the desire to communicate with others fuel the work we do. This is probably most true of those artists who work with autobiography, their own lived experience transmuted into image or storytelling—artists who pull their own masks off and use them to pan for universal gold. Performance is a process whose raw materials include emotion and experience—and when it clicks, honoring these in front of an audience is heady and sacred indeed.

> *What's the matter, baby. Are you shy? Haven't you ever been to a place like this before? The way it works is, you come into my booth and lock the door so we can be alone—then I can put on a show for you. It's five dollars for three minutes—that's not much, baby. You'd be amazed what can happen in three minutes. We could have a whole relationship in three minutes.*

After high school drama I fled from performance. I was a teenage thespian, as my parents used to proudly call me (though my mother once slipped and said "lesbian," not knowing just how prescient she was). Finally I had to face the moment the roles, which I'd gratefully embraced as a way to distance myself from my life, began to lead me back into my own self. This wasn't exactly why I fled, but neither was I ready for the introspection this evoked.

I fled to sex, another venue that offered escape and distraction coupled with deep opportunities for introspection and soul-searching. Now my "performances" were solitary or for an audience of one (or, during very dramatic times, two). Eventually I discovered a wildly exhibitionistic streak to my sexual enjoyment, which further linked my pleasure in sex to the pleasure I had once felt on stage. It was probably inevitable that those two sources of pleasure, attention, and transformative, communicative play would hook up: to put it another way, that I would come to find that in my life, the Bed is muse to the Stage, and vice versa.

> *Get comfortable if you want. I'm just going to move around a little—it gets cramped in this little booth. I could use a good stretch.* [Moving around sinuously, turning and bending slowly over to show the customer/audience my ass, running my hands over the cheeks, down the backs of my thighs. Turning to face forward again, kneeling right in front of the "glass" and cupping my breasts, stroking, looking at the customer]

Another way I see sex and performance as connected has to do with confidence: the way both the sexual being and the artist are challenged to stretch and to extend themselves to others, how deeply our achievements can be limited if courage and confidence fail us. How much deeper we can go when we don't let fear of creativity hobble us. When I see the tarot card that pictures the Fool dancing on a precipice, I see the challenge of both the artist and the lover. When I'm wearing my sex educator hat I constantly see people who have let fear of being abnormal, too "out there," or too emotionally exposed stifle their sexuality; conversely, a successful experience of edge-dancing shapes and hones our naked bravery.

More than one lover invited my exhibitionism out in sex play, and most did so patiently, so that my initial stage fright gave way to self-assurance. Eventually I took my newfound confidence (and the pleasure it brought) to a real, if secret, stage: a peep show booth. Here was my red velvet curtain, my audience, theater without scripts. It worked like this: I could be seen, framed by my curtain, from a hallway. From here I lured men into the booth for a "private show": an erotic improvisation based on the customer's fantasy. Unlike the disembodied voice of the phone fantasy worker, I was completely visible, and though I took a pseudonym, a peep show character who ostensibly masked my real identity, it was my body the customers saw and interacted with. Because the work was improvised and intimate, "Minx Manx" had to be more deeply sourced in my own sexuality and self than any character I'd ever played on the stage.

> *You can touch yourself too, baby. That's what we do in here. Go on, take your cock out if you want. Did you walk in here with any fantasies? What would you like to do if this glass weren't in the way? Stroke me like this? Run your hands all over my skin? Wait a minute, I have something to show you.* [Sitting back a little, more self-stroking, showing off; very slowly, bra comes off]

Backstage at the peep show a dozen women at a time sat before makeup mirrors creating their erotic characters: dykes with shaved heads became kittenish blondes, graduate students turned into leather-clad dominatrixes. Each character mixed fantasy with an archetype that would allow the peep show worker to access her own sexuality—at least enough of it to source a believable character. Many of my co-workers said they created characters to shield themselves from direct intimate contact with the customers. I, on the other hand, was fascinated by the intimacy, and found performing much hotter when I felt an interactive connection.

> *Look, my nipples get so hard when I stroke them just right. It's not a light touch, but it's not too hard, either. Just right. I can get so turned on just playing with my breasts. It's hot that you're watching me. Come on, take your cock out so I can watch you.* [Standing up again, legs apart, beginning to run fingertips under the seam of my panties]

Often customers would assume a character, too. Every type came in there to begin with (everybody male, anyway): suits who'd flip their neckties over their shoulders so they won't be stained with jizz when they get back to the office, young guys with their skateboards, men with buzzcuts from the military bases, old Chinese men who just want to stare. But often their fantasies involved a persona or scenario that took them away from their everyday selves: that was one attraction of the peep show, I am sure. Ordinary guys who probably didn't play any fancy sexual games at home would want to become submissives or dominants, play the role of a fourteen-year-old virgin or a cross-dressed slut. I was prepared with props and costumes, of course—dildos, vibrators, lingerie—but so were many of the customers, for whom the peep show represented perhaps the only opportunity in their lives to do erotic theater of their own.

> *Let's see you, honey. Stroke yourself off while I watch. Take it out so I can see it. Ohh, nice cock. Really pretty cock. Do people tell you that all the time, that you have a sexy cock? No? Well, they should.* [Abruptly all lights go out]
> *Oh, no, baby, the time is up! Would you like any more time? Just slide a bill in and the lights will come back on and we can play a little longer. Oh, thank you, honey.*

Sometimes the job was more sex education than stage. "Can I just look at your pussy?" one man in his seventies asked wistfully. "My own wife won't let me look at her pussy." Other times the customer had such a clear role in mind for me to play that all I

needed to do was channel the character: horny aunt, innocent Catholic schoolgirl. And sometimes roles were irrelevant: sexual connection through a pane of glass (which separated me spatially from
the customer) was hotter than I could ever have imagined. In the
course of a day's work I could appear in a dozen playlets, give
several men their first clear look at a clitoris, and have steamy
sexual encounters with a few more.

> *Okay, let's have some fun, shall we, baby? Let me get these
> panties out of the way. Did you come in here to look at my
> pussy? Did you ever get a really good look?* [Hooks fingers in
> panties' elastic again, pulls slowly down; as pubic hair starts to
> show, turns around and finishes, very slowly, showing off ass,
> kicking panties off, turning around to display naked pussy,
> legs open]
>
> *There she is, baby, my little puss—let me get up close. She
> sees your cock all hard on the other side of that glass. Let's
> stroke. Can I move right here over you? Good, because I'm
> going to touch myself and come right in front of you now.* [Begin-
> ning to masturbate, stroking pussy, belly, breasts, thighs]
>
> *Feels so good, baby, so hot with you watching me. Make
> your hand move on your cock so I can watch you. I love
> watching men jack off, showing off for me. That's right, stroke
> it, make it feel good. Ohhh, I've got to lie down, baby, so I can
> really do it.*

I knew right away I wanted to translate this experience to public
performance. In the peep show I was privileged to see secret visions
of sexual desire and fantasy played out over and over again; I knew
I had a front-row seat at one usually hidden aspect of sexual culture.
I met people I wanted to introduce audiences to. And I was very
curious about my ability to bring Minx (and myself) out of our little
glass booth and into a theater.

> *Come on, honey, work your cock. Watch how fast I go on my
> clit—have you ever seen a clit all hard and turned on? Look at
> me. Ohhh—so fucking good, so hot, showing you what I like to
> do to myself. Ohh, yeah . . .* [Light goes out again]

Ohh, baby, time's up! Next time you come see me we can play with my dildos.

Besides, the peep show is a microcosm of eroticism, desire, persona, the theatrical ritual of fantasy, and the very same sexual schizophrenia that creates the climate for peep shows in the first place. It's also a locus for the cultural gender malaise that says men pay for it and women dole it out, men expect women to be "good" and wish they were "bad" (and devalue them when they are). The peeps are a rich stew, and I want to stir it in public.

> [Note: Because the performance *Peep Show* relies on audience interaction, if the energy is right, I'll offer a dildo show instead of saying good-bye after the second three minutes is up; the point is to as closely as possible approximate the private peep show experience in a public venue, with the entire audience standing in for my customer, choosing which dildo I'll play with, etc. Audience members may also be encouraged to (from their seats or coming up front) engage me with their fantasies, which I'll talk through with them. At the "end" of the performance itself I may stay onstage, nude or in my lingerie, answering audience questions. The idea is to break the hermetic seal of the booth, so like a confessional, while at the same time reproducing it.]

I also want to contradict our tendency to take sex less than seriously: I know how many of my peep show visitors were surprised that I was well-spoken and thoughtful ("Why, you're smart!" said one), and I know how many theatergoers share the assumption that sexual explicitness and intelligence can't mix—look at how Annie Sprinkle's show *Post-Porn Modernist* charmed and confounded critics who expected no substance from an ex-porn star. It is critical—and I speak here as a sexologist, as an artist, and as a sexual being—that we undermine this tendency to see sex as a subject unworthy of serious study and creative expression. All this does is continue to marginalize sexuality, the sexually divergent, and each of our desires. It reinforces the schizophrenia that facilitates gender war, epidemics of sexually transmitted disease, and lives plagued by sexual dearth, misery, or simply boredom.

It is my intent, when I perform *Peep Show* for an audience who keep their hands out of their pants, to pose questions and shake assumptions about sex as much as to arouse and entertain. I want to reconstruct the private theater of the peep show in a public venue, inviting and challenging my audience to stand in the place of my customer, decontextualizing my "very private show . . . for your eyes only" and creating a voyeurism that informs as much as it inspires. Peep shows exist to feed sexual hunger. But the hunger that sexuality creates gnaws more in the brain than between our legs, and I would like to make a meal of that.

Exercises in Manual Dexterity: Making Porn Videos Work for Women

Sally Trash

I watch a lot of "adult movies," much to the perplexity of my friends. They ask me how on earth I can sit through that stuff—the repetition, the lack of foreplay, the bad hair styles. The trick is this: figure out a way to make porn work for you. All you need is a remote control and an understanding of what you like to look at. Here are a few tips, and some thoughts about the porn market.

HOW TO WATCH PORN VIDEOS

First of all, there isn't a lot of foreplay in mainstream vids. There are lots and lots of scenes of people *in a hurry to fuck*. Each position is short-lived, so that you-the-viewer gets variety. This means that you don't slip the cassette in the machine so that you can *get* horny, so that someone can take you by the hand from zero to sixty. You slip it in when you *are* horny.

Second, there are usually at least three segments to a film, scenes between different people in different combinations. All of these brave exhibitionists have their own personalities, bodies, gestures, comments, techniques, favorite positions, etc. Watch the film once throughout to see who keeps you interested. Remember her name and what she looks like so you can find her again on your next shopping/rental trip.

Third, films are heavily edited, so they won't unravel in a viewer's sexual real time. If you've ever tried to *make* a porn movie, you understand why editing is so important. Real sex in real time feels great because it fits the demands of that particular encounter.

Throughout the course of that interaction each player constantly adjusts to mood changes, body changes, and the physical layout of the playspace. To experience that is one thing; to watch it is another. I've made movies of my own encounters, all the details of which I remember clearly and enjoyed thoroughly. But when I watch them later those pauses for talk, lubing up, and rearranging furniture are not as interesting to me. I'm somewhere else and frankly, I just want to see the sex, the visual triggers that keep me excited. That is what porn makers generally provide: a pastiche of cues, not a document of events. So watch a porn flick like you would a flipbook of photographs, not like *Lawrence of Arabia.* Figure out what images your cunt's eye responds to. Do you like gynecology shots? Do you like watching whole bodies? Do you like that quirky little gesture the featured star makes with her mouth? Go back to the shots that turned you on—those are the reason you got the tape. Those are the images that, when you're teetering right on the edge, will send you hurtling down the other side.

If you don't like the background music, somebody's voice, or a particular string of comments, *turn the sound off.* The music can suffer in these movies when it's not made by musicians—musicians cost too much, and home synthesizers are too easy to play in loops, over and over and over again. Put on your own music, something with a bit of juice to it. If you are turned off by an actor's verbal persona, don't listen to it. If there's a voice-over that bugs you, *definitely* don't listen to it. It has been laid in after the sex took place, so it has nothing to do with the scene itself, and in the case of some of the German-made movies out there, it *will* offend you. The point is that you're using this vid to have sex with: focus on the stuff you like, ignore the stuff you don't. There's plenty of fodder there for a healthy deconstructionist critique of porn, but right now your life is hanging on the end of your clit, not on the left lobe of your brain.

Caveat: The porn viewer's best friend is her remote control. It's the difference between a slow doze on the Broadway bus and a curb jump on a Harley. Fast-forward when you're bored, slow-mo when you're onto something. A personal fave is the "out" slide in a close-up penetration scene, when the skin at the bottom of a woman's cunt is pulled and stretched out. That sends me, and I'll watch it repeatedly in slow motion, real time, frame by frame.

SOME THOUGHTS ON THE MARKET

If you haven't figured this out already, I'm a big fan of close-up shots. It seems that savvy filmmakers, those who would like women as well as men to watch their movies, are also fans. I figure this is the case for two reasons. One is that the majority of mainstream porn, male- and female-directed, is made for heterosexual audiences. Women directors know that straight women don't get a very good view of their cunts during sex, and they don't get to see other women's bodies if they're not having sex with them. Close-ups provide that opportunity for female viewers. Second, a good close-up of any part of the body gives the viewer a sense of intimacy, sexual intimacy. I personally don't need an extended plotline dripping with romance, and full development of each character, to satisfy my need for some kind of feeling of connection with the actors and cameraperson. And I deeply resent the stereotype that women viewers do need those storylines to warm the cockles of their hearts, in preparation for watching sex. The actors you are watching in a movie often don't know how to act that stuff out anyway. But they do, usually, love sex. And loving sex means, among other things, fully appreciating the body of the person they are having sex with. A close-up is a fairly graphic way of showing that.

I can usually pick out a female-made movie right away if it includes lots of close-ups. That's about the only gender distinction I can safely make when it comes to porn. Most of the films I've rented were made by men, because that's what dominates the video rental market. And men have covered much of what is possible with a few actors, a camera, and the parameters of Canadian obscenity laws: slow-touchy-feely sex, fast-action-panic sex, indoors, outdoors, verbal, nonverbal, funny, serious, etc. It's harder for me to generalize about movies made by women. I haven't seen enough of them, and because I live in the faith that if enough were out there movie for movie, genre for genre, there would be few differences. Some people will disagree with me on that point. I hope for a day when that can be tested, when women manage the porn world in the same numbers as men do, when their products are as available as those created by men.

It is also important to remember that the director's most powerful impact on the movie she or he will make is likely to be the choice of actors. Players are often chosen (and watched) for their unique body quirks and fucking techniques. They are specialists, and are appreciated by directors and audiences as such. Any good director makes a point of highlighting that very fact. Camerawork (e.g., whole bodies versus close-ups) and editing (e.g., to include or cut out the transitions between sexual moments) are also significant to the feel of a movie, and aspects where a director's personal preferences will be apparent. But the viewer's use of a video, especially if she uses it in the way I've suggested above, can dominate those aspects of direction to fit her own preferences. It's the viewer who chooses where to linger or fast-forward, so that she is, in effect, creating her own movie to watch. What endures in all of this cutting and pasting is still the content of the movie, and the content is the actor's style and body.

So when people ask me about the emerging role of women directors in porn, and the significance that may have for the products we rent, my response is as follows: Women dominate the pool of porn actors in the biz, and as actors their impact is powerful. If more women participated as directors there would be significant changes in the mechanics of the industry, the things we as viewers would not necessarily see (e.g., the types of contracts drawn up, the circumstances of filming, etc.). In terms of the movies themselves, and with all due respect to women directors, there are many more factors that determine the personal appeal of a movie than the gender of the person directing it. Where real breakthroughs are going to happen in the porn video biz is not so much in terms of who directs them, but rather, who comes up with new ideas on how to watch them. Think about it: one huge breakthrough was the retailing of porn on home video cassettes. This enables the viewer to watch films in a context she prefers, to watch them when she feels like watching them, to engage in whatever activity she feels like while watching, and to tailor the film to her interests by simply fiddling with a few knobs. It does require cash to rent the movie and if necessary the VCR, and it does still mean a foray into a porn outlet.

But let's face it, that's still a relatively inexpensive date. Many ma-and-pa, friendly video stores have adult sections (so you don't have to wander through the inner city to find it), and whenever I've treated male porn shoppers and vendors with respect I've received it back. I've had more hassles buying clothes at Le Chateau than I've ever had renting vids at Alpha.

I spoke to someone recently who is involved in a new development in interactive porn-watching. The company creates a series of porn videos, one of which the consumer buys and takes home. The consumer then calls the pay-per-minute phone number on the jacket, an operator answers, and both operator and consumer put copies of the same video onto their VCRs. They then watch it together, talking about what they are watching in whatever way they both feel comfortable. They might talk as operator and consumer enjoying a flick together, as expert showing novice the joys of porn, or as two invented personas peripherally connected to the sex they are watching. The possibilities are multiple, the social dimension the key. Many people are uncomfortable watching porn because they are not sure how the visual component of sex fits into their lives. This service acknowledges the complexity of porn and our reactions to it, and allows for an "expert" to share some ideas with a novice. Other people are very familiar with watching porn because it is the main component of their sex lives, other factors preventing them from having social, interactive sex. This service puts the two together: social exchange and visual sex. I think it's brilliant, brilliant, brilliant.

Fulfilling porn use, like satisfying sex, doesn't necessarily happen "naturally." Both are endeavors that require a certain decisiveness, consciousness, and risk of failure in order to figure out what your buttons are and what will push them. If you haven't already, try taking porn into your own hands, so to speak. As a close personal friend once said, porn won't come to you, but you can come to it.

Caution: Sharp Object

Tristan Taormino

Every inch of me is covered in blue Saran wrap, and I must be suffocating. The boy in the bed with me has named himself after two American icons, part sex kitten, part serial killer. He might look like a young Alice Cooper if he didn't look so much like Pee-Wee Herman's psycho-sinister twin with long black hair shiny but thirsty from all the dyeing, bright red lips, black ink-drawing tattoos over creamy vampire skin, and dangly girl-fingers encased with sharp silver rings. He looks at me with eyes defined by thick black slashes; I gaze back through the glossy plastic. He's skinny, so skinny he looks like a high school boy in cut-off jeans and he acts like one. This is that young alternative rockerboy who commits perverse acts on stage, fresh from his arrest in Florida for getting naked during a show. Yeah, he knows he's a star, but he's shy with me. (He won't let me see his dick, even though he's going to be naked in the photos.) I am already naked, except for one ripped pink stocking alone on my left thigh, pussy freshly shaved, my black eyeliner and dark red lipstick (to match his) carefully smeared and messed until I look like I've been savaged or ravaged, or maybe raped. He covers himself in front of my eyes, innocently twirling the telephone cord. Who is the kitten and who is the killer? He is the boy just interviewed in that music mag where they want to hear about his influences, when he'll be in the studio again, and all he wants to talk about is sex and his obsession with *erotic asphyxiation*. He likes to choke girls while he fucks them. The photographer is standing over the bed, checking the light. My tits are too bright. He asks me again if I feel all right, if everything's cool. I say yeah, and he tells me okay, then I'm going to start shooting. Look dead, he says. But keep your eyes open.

I'm full from our three-hour dinner; my insides are dripping of pure virgin olive oil, swimming in sweet red wine. I think we're going home, but we're suddenly walking the opposite direction from the car toward *that* street, and then we're walking past the neon lights and windowless walls: xxx live girls nude girls girl-girl sex shows xxx. She knows the place she wants to go, a place where the doorman won't smirk or give us a hard time or yell "fuckin' dykes!" at us. But I forget we're passing tonight, her in a dark double-breasted suit, me in my short flowered dress. We're a boy-girl couple looking for adventure. Inside our own private booth, I see her, this girl that's going to dance for us. I wonder if I ever looked that cute perky tired annoyed ready sexy when I danced. I wonder how many times my date has cruised the shows, how many times she has come here to this one, how many times she has seen her, this one. But I don't have time to think all of it through because she's messing with me, rubbing her hands between my legs, pushing the dress up while she watches the dancer wink at her. Does she know she's winking at another girl? Or does she just think it's a handsome man out on a date with a much younger girl? A girl who was asked for ID at the door, thought to be sixteen, actually almost twenty-four, but feeling sixteen, like a nymphomaniac teenage girl needing to be fucked all the time. I spread my legs for her. She knows I want it 'cause I always want it—need it—from her. She slides back my wet panties, can't take her eyes off the girl, can't take her hands off me. I'm pretending she's never done this before, never taken a girl here. I close my eyes so they can watch each other and I can watch it all in my head.

The blond is not as girlie as she looks: bleached-out, ratty hair cut in different lengths with intense black roots; pale and perfect skin, slightly flushed to match her soft, pink, fuzzy sweater stretched over touchable breasts; deep brandy-colored lips overdrawn and painted outside the lines; lace-up boots over ripped fishnets. Drinking a martini straight from the chrome shaker. She and her rough-and-tough-looking bass player are shooting a threesome. I'm naked again, except for white knee socks and shiny red patent leather Mary Janes. The blond kneels in front of me as if she's about to eat my hairless pussy between spread legs while the bass player stands behind me, holds my arms behind my back and watches. The bass player is shorter, with bright orange hair cut in a shaggy flip, a sort of Tori Spelling-on-speed kind of look. Flashes blind my eyes, and I can't see anything, only hear her in my ear. Telling me how much she likes to ass-fuck girls, girlie girls like me, how perfect my lips are, how fuckable my ass is, how much she wants to stick her tongue up inside me. The blond moves closer to me, and I wonder if these two are lovers. Yes, they certainly could be. They'll go home tonight and fuck, the bass player whispering things to the blond, or the blond will think of eating my cunt while she's eating hers and get off that way. No. The orange-haired one sneaks the test prints from the shoot into the bathroom, covers her girlfriend's body, and jerks off in the middle of the night to me, my naked body held together by her, spread apart for her lover.

We meet at a club and I'm all dolled up for her in a silver lamé babydoll dress, thigh highs, black high-heel lace-up boots, and the silver chain collar, locked around my neck since the day she put it there. It's a leatherboy bar, so I'm the only one in a dress, and she likes that, likes it so much that she leads me to the corner bathroom, pushes the door closed, leaving it slightly open, and takes her dick out, makes me suck it from on my knees on the cold dirty bathroom floor which smells like piss and cigarettes. I take its length in my mouth as she pushes herself into me, shoving her dick down my throat, so I can feel it scrape the roof of my mouth. There's lipstick on the condom when she pulls herself out of me and lifts me up on the sink facing her, so she can kiss me, bite my lips, suck on my neck. She tastes like smoke and beer. I'm not wearing any underwear, she discovers, as she lifts my skirt up to see what's hers. I'm slick and swollen and my legs and lips are spread for her. She rubs herself at my opening, presses the head into my clit, pushes there as I steady myself on the tiny sink. I know that there are boys right outside, peering through the six-inch space, growing hard in their denim and leather, stroking themselves at the sight of such a capable top with such a big dick. I'm sure they all want her to fuck them and make them suck her, but I'm daddy's little girl and all they can do is peek through the opening and listen through the door and imagine. I can see the whole scene in the filthy mirror on the back of the door. Behind the door, their eyes and their bulges are watching me.

He looks like a freak: straggly brown hair, deep-set eyes no describable color, and a wizened apple-head face, incredible lines marking the flesh of his now-kicked heroin habit, late nights cutting himself on stage, touring and trashing the clubs he's played in. I've tied him to a chair with thick black rope, the cameras are rolling, a song I've never heard before is playing really loud. He's talking, saying some shit about how nice my tits are, how he wants to eat my pussy, and I don't want him to talk anymore. I want him to shut that smart mouth of his, shut the fuck up, so I slap him as hard as my hand will let me. While his skin is still stinging, I pry his fat, stupid mouth open and shove a fluorescent ball gag in there. I buckle the leather strap too tight around his head and make sure to get some little pieces of hair caught in it, so he winces and struggles. Then it begins, my favorite part. Saliva runs down his chin, neck, and chest. He is salivating like the dog he is, drooling uncontrollably like the sick freak he is. He needs to be smacked, fuck it, he wants to be, but most important, I want to pound his face until he cries. Each black leather lash of the whip is braided with knotted ends. I begin slowly, establish a rhythm that will falsely lull him as I beat his chest, and when I feel like it, I move my arm just slightly, so that a few lashes graze his neck and if he flinches they will hit his face, wet with spit. I know it hurts, I can see the red welts raising up on his skin, and he can't scream or ask me to stop or tell me to. His eyes plead with me. He's asking for it. I'm high from fucking this motherfucker and if someone yelled "cut" or "stop," I didn't hear it.

When I come home from a long shoot, she's got her dick on and the lights off. She's jerking off to the glow of a porn movie with her cock in one hand and the remote in the other, watching this big blond guy sodomize her favorite brunette. I know I'm next. She takes her eyes off the screen for a moment to watch me put my stuff down and strip. I kiss her. She says I smell like plastic and darkroom chemicals. She tells me I'm a slut, *dirty*, and I better scrub my body good, get all the sleaze off me, because she's not going to touch me until all the makeup is off, the marks of a day's work are gone, and I'm fresh and clean and *hers* again. She wants to watch me do it, but she wants to watch the action on the screen more. So I go to the dark room alone, and I'm glad she has let me because I need the solitude, the hot water, the sound of it flooding the bathtub. When I climb in, the water scorches my skin, but I like to feel the stings in the places I've been hit, the aches of the muscles I've strained. I want to look at my skin wet and flushed, feel my pussy under my hand as I jerk off, but there will be a knock at the door soon. And when the lights come on, I'll be ready to dance for her again.

Hot Lights

Kevin Killian

For Clifford Hengst

For long stretches of time every day, I kept my body inside my clothes, but sometimes it broke out and made a fool out of "me," the me I wanted to represent to the outside world. Hungry for heat and light, my body rolled itself out of hiding at the snap of a klieg light, and this scared me. It certainly ruined my chances for ever running for public office, and I suppose limited my options in other ways. For everything one's body does limits or directs the rest of one's future. I met Jig Johnson in the early 1970s, when I was a college student, high as a kite but perpetually short on cash. Drugs were cheap then, so was liquor, but since I had only a job as a grocery clerk, I was always on the make, trying to stay alive in New York. Four times a week I would sell my blood, traipsing from bank to blood bank all over midtown with a sprightly gait that tires me now just to think of it. A pal at school told me, sotto voce, of a man who paid students large sums for acting in porn loops. He said these loops, in primitive color, badly lit, could be seen in various raucous Times Square peep shows, where weirdos dropped a quarter in a slot and a lead shield shot up into the wall, unveiling a twist of naked limbs and cocks. At some random time, say, five minutes, the shield descended again implacably.

"Uh . . ." "Duh . . ." I weighed the pros and cons in my head like the figure of Libra on *Perry Mason.* Trying to figure out what would be right for me, but not thinking very clearly. I was naive to the nth degree. First of all, thanks to a steady diet of so-called "soft" porn, I didn't imagine that "acting" in porn would involve having sex in front of a camera. I had never actually seen a hard porn film. I had the suspicion that the actors might take off their clothes, might kiss, might pretend to have a kind of sex. Cynically I thought everything else was faked, as in Hollywood films. "Special effects." I remember, around that time, reading current discussions of gay representation in the media. I was taking "creative writing" at school, so I felt personally involved with the debate, and felt obliged to make all my gay characters positive images. Oh, amid what fog of delusion I walked Manhattan, straining my brains to think of ways to make everyone lovable. . . . How would my appearance in a porn film affect the representation of my tribe? I couldn't work it out. When I called Jig Johnson from a public phone in the lobby of school, the line was busy so I went to my French class. After ninety minutes of Rimbaud and Verlaine I tried the number again. Ring. Ring. "Hello?" That's when I started to panic. Luckily Johnson was businesslike and really together, as if to compensate for the stupid qualms of the guys who were probably always calling him up to feed their habits. He asked me if I was ready to play with the big boys. "Sure." He asked if I was free that evening for my audition. There was a bottle of Southern Comfort in my pocket. Secretively I downed some, then sifted my little pile of thoughts like Brian Wilson playing in that sandbox. "What time?" I said, nodding out.

In his apartment, he held my cock in his hands and watched it swell up, like one of those time-lapse photography miracles on public TV. I stared down too, feeling the simultaneous pride and shame of an unbidden erection. Presently, when I was hard as a bone, Johnson slapped my cock, told me to get down on my hands and knees on the floor. "Head on the side of the bed," he called out, from the other room, the room where my clothes were, I hoped. On the pinstriped gamy mattress, stained with a dozen men's come, I lay my head flat, praying I'd make it through my audition.

He dug a flash camera out of the hamper and dangled it close to my nose. God knows what I looked like, what distorted expression was frozen on my dumb face. Then the flash exploded and the chemical smell of the early Polaroid film filled the squalid room. As I remained there, stiff and blinking, he moved behind me to crouch down between my legs. I felt him trying to spread my knees, so I helped, trying to oblige. I don't know, did I do the right thing? I felt a wet hand slither down my butt, down its crack, and I wondered if he was going to screw me. I kept thinking, *I'm playing with the big boys now.*

But he told me he just wanted a picture of my asshole.

And there I was thinking, *what, no sex?* I remember being assaulted by my own thoughts and my feelings of unworthiness, while the Polaroid started to whirl. Presently he threw down two pictures in front of my face: grainy shots, in lurid color, of my demented face, and my tight little red hole, like a bullet hole in the middle of what seemed an absurdly overstated butt.

"You'll be perfect," he said, and I wondered what perfection meant, if such banal evidences gave me so much pause. "You can dress now," he said, in a gentler tone. I covered my crotch with my hands as I walked out of the room. Like a little boy surprised. Suddenly I realized that porn acting involved actual sex captured on film. It just came to me in a revelation like St. Paul on the way to Damascus—a blinding light. "Far out," I thought, for I was always ready to have sex with other guys, but at the same time the thought of film's perpetuity unnerved me. It's one thing to reflect that, no matter how much of a mess she became, we can always think of Judy Garland as sweet sixteen singing in the cornfield; it was another to consider that, in a certain sense, I would always be a nineteen-year-old nitwit with a cock up my ass and a pot-induced glaze in my eyes. I found my clothes, undisturbed, and jammed them on willy-nilly. Johnson produced a bent card, with an address scribbled on the back. He tied my necktie for me, absently, helped me tuck in my shirt. He smelled of some lemony scent like the floor wax my mother used at home on her kitchen floor. He was indescribably dapper, everything I thought of when I thought of the words, "New York." Even the points of his collar were perfect white triangles, stiff, formal, like watercress sandwiches cut in half. I felt like a slob in front of him, could hardly look him in the eye. If I had, oh dear, what pity or contempt would I have seen there? Or was I his mirror, his younger self, a self without a single social grace, no ease? I steeled up my courage and insisted that I wouldn't play an effeminate hysterical hairdresser in his loop, a type gay activists were deploring in the great debate. "You won't be playing any type," he said—probably baffled. "You'll just be yourself." Swell, except I didn't know who that self could be. In looks I resembled a slightly

beefed-up version of the Disney actress Hayley Mills—very an-
drogynous, in the spirit of the times—and my voice had hardly
broken, so I was still prone to embarrassing squeaks that made me
wish the floor would open up. So—so whatever . . .

At the front door another guy waited, in old army fatigues, and as
if on a whim, Johnson had me unbutton the guy's pants and suck his
cock for a minute. I thought about it for maybe ten seconds, then
agreed, for auditioning had made me horny, and until this possibility of contact, I felt utterly unattractive. "Hi," the guy said.
"Hmhhrw!" said I. He was my age, nineteen, or just about, with
chalky white skin and hair dyed orange as Tropicana. I massaged
his muscled thighs as I bobbed up and down in his lap. "That's
fine," said Jig Johnson. "You can stop now." My costar, whose
name turned out to be Guy, shot a pitying glance at Johnson.
"Where you recruiting now, Jig?" he said shakily. "Port Authority?"
Johnson smiled and caressed Guy's orange sideburn in an absent
avuncular manner, while Guy yawned and gradually reeled his dick
back in his khakis. "There'll be six of you tomorrow," Johnson said.
"Meet us at ten o'clock, Kevin."

"Okay," I stuttered, "and thanks, Mr. Johnson."

Guy called after me, "You're too good for this son of a bitch."
Right then I kind of fell in love a bit. I set my alarm over and over
again, took a dozen showers.

Of the actual filming I recall very little. I mounted the stairs of a
dilapidated building a block from Broadway—had the space once
been a dance studio? Big quiet room, torn blinds drawn to the floor,
a room scattered with the kind of furniture college students leave
behind in their dorm rooms after they graduate. There was a steady
roar in my head, a dull roar like a subway station, a roar which rose
as I met my other costars and first saw the camera, a big box with a
red light beaming underneath to show we were "on." Had they
invented videotape back then? I don't think so. Here film itself was
the precious, expensive thing, to be parceled out in stingy dear bits.
I asked for my script, to give me something to read, to give me
something to look at instead of all those distracting bodies sliding
out of street clothes. I did notice that one guy had a shorter dick than
mine, so I butched it up in all our scenes together, I'm no fool, I
thought, one less thing to obsess about. . . .

"Jig, Kevin wants to take a look at the script." First a blank look, then a laugh, then everyone laughed at my naïvete. Guy, my costar, patted my back consolingly, long white pats that brought the sweat dripping down into the crack of my ass. Nice guy. None of us had scripts per se, but there were scratch marks all over the carpet, drawn with chalk I suppose, of where we would stand at various intervals, usually down on one knee. Mystifying marks like the arbitrary symbols in the Lascaux caves. Johnson told us to make up all our dialogue, since another gang of boys would dub us over in a different situation, probably a different city. Everyone was hard, stiff, unbelievably so, and when the hot lights bore down on my erection it gleamed like topaz, under a light coating of mineral oil, and I said to myself, I'd take that home with me! *I'd* pay money to see that! *Who's* attached to this rod of steel?

It—my rod of steel—twitched; and great shadows leaped and fell across Guy's startled, tiny face underneath: he resembled a still from some excellent Maya Deren film like *Meshes in the Afternoon.*

One guy, Charles, long blond hair like Fabio's, touch of a blond goatee at the base of his spine, spent hours bent over the back of a large sofa, getting fucked over and over, and his only line was "Mount me"—*that* stuck with me. In the morning his asshole was a thin slit, moist, exquisitely puckered, but by late afternoon it looked like a red rubber ball, torn in half, and pierced with blood, sunk deep within. Most of all I remember the heat of the lights, how huge lights two feet wide threatened to blow the fuses of the entire apartment building, and how when their shutters opened a giant click sound rocked the whole room. These white-hot domes, trained on one's skin, were like the great eyes of God the poet Jack Spicer wrote of in *Imaginary Elegies.* They see everything, even under the skin where your thoughts are. Your dirty little thoughts. You can take off all your clothes and pretend to be "naked," but you are still Kevin Killian from Smithtown, Long Island, with all the petty details that denotes. And yet at the same time the heat made me feel languorous, forgetful, like Maria Montez at the top of some Aztec staircase—dangerous, as though there were nothing beyond the circle of white—no audience, no society, only oneself and the red or purple or black hard-on that floats magically to the level of one's lips. I suppose all actors must feel the same way in some part of their being—that the camera's eye represents the eye of God, which at the same time judges all and, threateningly, withholds all judgment till time turns off.

We poured out onto the street at sunset, tired and spent, yakking it up. We would never be stars I thought. No one would ever see this "loop." And I was glad, but sorry too. I asked if anyone knew the name of the picture. No one did. (Charlie said they should call it *Saddlesore*.) It didn't really have a name, and as such, I thought, it had no real existence. Just six guys fucking and sucking. We said we would all meet in six months at a Times Square grindhouse for the premiere. Auld acquaintance. I tried visualizing our putative audience and words popped into my head: "a bunch of perverts"—shady men in black trenchcoats, visiting conventioneers touring the louche side of gay New York. Nobodies in fact. "Bye, dudes." "Later." "Adios." I took away more money than I'd ever made in my life—a hundred dollars, except Johnson took back like three dollars because he bought us some lunch—beer and Kentucky Fried Chicken. At the same time, I read some interview with Lou Reed: asked whether he thought homosexuality was increasing, he replied to the effect that, "It's a fad, but people will tire of it, because eventually you have to suck cock or get your ass fucked." I reflected that I had in one fell swoop ruined my chance to be president, earned ninety-seven dollars, made a new boyfriend, kind of, solidified my connections with the entertainment world, had some great sex, and still I felt utterly ashamed of my own specularity, my need to see and be seen. I came, onto the face and chest of a boy, and my semen seemed to spatter and fry, before my eyes, as though his body were the very skillet of love, such was the wattage of those hot lights.

I remember walking around Columbus Circle looking for things to buy with my money, and feeling disappointed that there are no stores there, only pretzel vendors and hot dog carts, so I bought a pretzel and a hot dog, and stood with one foot curled around the ironwork fence at Central Park South, watching the crowd. Wondering if anyone could "tell." My wallet felt fat, expansive, as though my money might grow to enormous size and eat the whole fucking city. I was so filled up with energy I thought I could walk all the way uptown to Guy's neighborhood, then just kind of drop in, rekindle our newfound intimacy, lick that dead-white skin from the nape of his neck to the puncture wounds inside his arm. . . . I slid into a bar on Sixth Avenue, pondering desire, Guy, money, and guilt. Had I let down my tribe by playing a part which wasn't actually a part per se, but couldn't therefore be a "positive" one? Wish I could go back and console my younger self, rub his young shoulders, explicate latter-day porn theory to cheer him up. And also get him to cut back on all that drinking! At once the most and least ironic of art forms, pornography undercuts the performative authenticity of penetration with oh, just lashes of mad camp. Its greatest stars, like those of performance art, are the biggest dopes in the world; its most discerning fans those, like my present-day self, who feel ourselves beyond representation for one imaginary reason or another. I stepped into a liquor store on 82nd for a bottle of Seagram's 7, knowing I'd find an answer in its rich musky depths. On the way out I saw a phone booth, and I called Guy, who had scrawled his number backward up my thigh from the back of my knee to the juncture of my balls. "I know it's not six months yet," I said, "but I was thinking—" "I can still taste your dick in my mouth," he said—an encouraging sign, or so I thought, but instead he hung up on me, and I felt a blush rise right up to my temples. I thought everyone was staring at the dumb boy on the dumb phone who just got the brushoff. The glare of judgment burning me like lasers through my cool.

I kept thinking, I'm wearing way too many clothes! And I fled. Finally night fell and I looked up at the moon that shone over Morningside Heights, its white soft beam so limpid, full of the poetry of Shakespeare and the Caribbean and George Eliot—the antithesis I suppose of the hot lights I had grown to need. How relaxed, how relieved I now felt, in the white moonlight. Relieved of the chore of playing with the big boys. My clothes seemed to fit again, I became myself. The moon's fleecy lambency corralled my pieces and relinked us, we joined "hands" as it were and sang and danced in a circle, like "We Are the World" or some such filler. I became Kevin Killian. Did I make a mistake?

Index

Order Your Own Copy of
This Important Book for Your Personal Library!

STRATEGIC SEX
Why They Won't Keep It in the Bedroom

_____ in hardbound at $39.95 (ISBN:1-56023-969-7)

_____ in softbound at $14.95 (ISBN: 1-56023-970-0)

COST OF BOOKS_____

OUTSIDE USA/CANADA/
MEXICO: ADD 20%_____

POSTAGE & HANDLING_____
(US: $3.00 for first book & $1.25
for each additional book)
Outside US: $4.75 for first book
& $1.75 for each additional book)

SUBTOTAL_____

IN CANADA: ADD 7% GST_____

STATE TAX_____
(NY, OH & MN residents, please
add appropriate local sales tax)

FINAL TOTAL_____
(If paying in Canadian funds,
convert using the current
exchange rate. UNESCO
coupons welcome.)

☐ **BILL ME LATER:** ($5 service charge will be added)
(Bill-me option is good on US/Canada/Mexico orders only;
not good to jobbers, wholesalers, or subscription agencies.)

☐ Check here if billing address is different from
shipping address and attach purchase order and
billing address information.

Signature_____

☐ **PAYMENT ENCLOSED: $**_____

☐ **PLEASE CHARGE TO MY CREDIT CARD.**

☐ Visa   ☐ MasterCard   ☐ AmEx   ☐ Discover
☐ Diners Club
Account #_____

Exp. Date_____

Signature_____

Prices in US dollars and subject to change without notice.

NAME _____

INSTITUTION _____

ADDRESS _____

CITY _____

STATE/ZIP _____

COUNTRY _____ COUNTY (NY residents only) _____

TEL _____ FAX _____

E-MAIL_____
May we use your e-mail address for confirmations and other types of information? ☐ Yes   ☐ No

Order From Your Local Bookstore or Directly From
The Haworth Press, Inc.
10 Alice Street, Binghamton, New York 13904-1580 • USA
TELEPHONE: 1-800-HAWORTH (1-800-429-6784) / Outside US/Canada: (607) 722-5857
FAX: 1-800-895-0582 / Outside US/Canada: (607) 772-6362
E-mail: getinfo@haworthpressinc.com
PLEASE PHOTOCOPY THIS FORM FOR YOUR PERSONAL USE.